SECOND EDITION

Crystal Cove
COTTAGES

Seaside Morning by John Cosby
(oil on canvas, 48 x 60, 2002)

SECOND EDITION

Crystal Cove
COTTAGES

Islands in Time on the California Coast

written by Karen E. Steen

historic collections by Laura Davick

artistic collections by Meriam Braselle

principal photography by John Connell

foreword by Jean Stern

NEWPORT COAST, CALIFORNIA

Second edition 2017, Crystal Cove Conservancy

Text copyright © 2005 by Karen E. Steen, Laura Davick and Meriam Braselle
Original photographs copyright © 2005 by John Connell
Part of this text was adapted from an article written by Karen E. Steen, published in the February 2002 issue of *Metropolis*.
Page 157 constitutes a continuation of the copyright page.

All rights reserved. No part of this book may be reproduced in any form without written permission from the publisher.

Library of Congress Cataloging-in-Publication Data available.

ISBN 978-0-692-93214-8

Manufactured in China.

Second edition updates by Buchanan Brand + Design
First edition design by General Working Group: Geoff Kaplan & Kim West

Originally published: San Francisco, Chronicle Books, 2005 - 2016
ISBN 0-8118-4768

Crystal Cove Conservancy
#5 Crystal Cove
Newport Coast, California 92657

www.CrystalCove.org

The High Road by Michael Obermeyer
(oil on canvas, 20 x 16, 2001).

A View from Crystal Cove by Calvin Liang
(oil on canvas, 12 x 16, 2002).

Contents

Preface	8
Foreword	10
Introduction	12
Chapter 1 Unspoiled Vistas: The Cove before 1917	19
Plein Air Painters in Laguna Beach and Crystal Cove	30
Cottage #00: The Office	42
Cottage #2: The Davick Cottage	46
Chapter 2 Silent Films and Palm Fronds: 1917 to 1940	49
Cottage #13: The Beaches Cottage	64
Cottage #7: The Carter Cottage	66
Chapter 3 Every Night Was Saturday Night: 1941 to 1962	69
Cottage #34: The Japanese Schoolhouse	86
Cottage #46: The Store	88
Chapter 4 An Island in Time: 1963 to 1979	91
Cottage #14: The McCloskey Cottage	112
Cottage #27: The Rowland Cottage	114
Chapter 5 A Modern-Day Village: 1980 to 2001	117
Cottage #11: The Gabriel Cottage	142
Cottage #15: The Whistle Stop	144
The Future of Crystal Cove	146
Bibliography	154
Credits	157
Acknowledgments	158

Preface

The first edition of *Crystal Cove Cottages: Islands in Time on the California Coast* was originally published by Chronicle Books from 2005 to 2016. The authors—Meriam Braselle, Karen Steen, and Laura Davick, each with their own personal connections to this iconic landscape—came together to help document this important story so future generations would come to love and appreciate Crystal Cove as they have. This is a love story about the families that built these cottages and the spirit that still exists in them today. Meriam is a *plein air* painter and former resident of the Abalone Point community that once sat at the south end of Crystal Cove State Park. Karen and her family have deep roots that go back to the tent-camping era of the cove. For me, Crystal Cove is my past, present, and future. My parents and their families were tent campers at the cove, and it's here that they met, fell in love, and married. The Davicks called Cottage #2 home for 40 years. As founder of the organization created to rescue Crystal Cove, now known as the Crystal Cove Conservancy, I believe that these historic cottages are one of Orange County's most important cultural and historic assets.

This love story is still evolving, which is why we decided to publish a second edition of this book—to raise awareness of the ongoing preservation efforts and life-long stewardship that will always be necessary for this treasure called Crystal Cove. The story of the cove, just like the cove itself, must be preserved for future generations.

The Crystal Cove Conservancy is dedicated to protecting this rare piece of California history through a unique social enterprise model, working in partnership with California State Parks. This model allows the conservancy to develop innovative educational programs that bring the cove's rich environmental, artistic, and cultural significance alive for students and visitors, all while supporting the preservation of miles of precious California coastline. The completion of the final phase of restoration, rehabilitating the cottages on the north end of the beach, will forever preserve this one remaining untouched place in the sun.

For this reason, Karen, Meriam. and I have donated all proceeds of this book to support the mission of the Crystal Cove Conservancy.

To become a part of this story and the legacy that lives on at Crystal Cove, please visit the Crystal Cove Conservancy at www.CrystalCove.org.

Laura Davick
Founder and Vice President
Crystal Cove Conservancy

Jesse Powell's *Picket Fence*
(oil on canvas, 11 x 14, 2003)
won first place at the 2003 Crystal Cove
Alliance Plein Air Invitational.

Preface

Foreword

Crystal Cove

is a breathtaking bit of Eden, one of the most beautiful inlets along the Southern California coast. For several millennia it was home to undisturbed coastal flora and fauna, prior to the arrival of Native Americans who, for thousands of years, benefited from its beauty and bounty.

In the twentieth century, Crystal Cove entered the lore of American cinema as the vibrant and pristine setting for a number of early Hollywood movies. Starting in 1917 with the silent film version of *Treasure Island*, the cove's unique beauty became South Seas and Caribbean backdrops in numerous pirate and swashbuckler movies. In simulation of these tropical sites, film crews constructed a number of small reed shacks, thatched them with palm fronds, and planted tall coconut palms. Combined with the raw beauty of the cove, these movie sets created a convincing atmosphere for the filmmakers. One of these film sets later became one of the cove's first cottages.

Starting in the 1920s, people who had routinely camped at Crystal Cove began to build additional structures with whatever building materials they could secure. Soon, a small colony arose with a few families living there year-round. This was commonplace along the Southern California coast in the early part of the twentieth century, and it eventually led to the creation of numerous seaside villages and small towns. Crystal Cove belonged to the formidable Irvine Ranch, and aside from the small cottages, the cove remained mostly undeveloped. Today, the cove is one of the last remaining examples of early 20th century Southern California beach vernacular architecture.

Just as the cove drew the attention of Hollywood, it also attracted painters as early as the first decade of the twentieth century. The noted California Impressionist William Wendt (1865-1946) first visited the area in the late 1890s. His majestic painting *Crystal Cove* from 1912 shows the distinctive beach and hills in their natural state prior to the arrival of the filmmakers. By contrast, Arthur G. Rider (1886-1975), who painted the cove in the late 1920s, clearly shows the first structure built at Crystal Cove, now the Visitor Center.

Over the past century, Crystal Cove has been favored by artists of all persuasions, from *plein air* and realist to modern and abstract. Today, Crystal Cove continues to attract painters who seek to capture its unique charm and beauty. The distinguished artists of the Laguna Plein Air Painters Association and the Southern California Plein Air Painters Association can often be seen painting at the cove. Their striking paintings are a popular attraction at the Crystal Cove State Park Interpretive Store and Gallery, and many are lovingly taken home by visitors to remind them of the idyllic time they spent at the cove.

As executive director of the Irvine Museum Collection, I have sought out rare examples of paintings of the cove to include in our exhibitions of the works of California Impressionist painters executed from 1890 to about 1940. Very few artists painted Crystal Cove prior to about 1910. It appears more often in the works of the California Scene painters, working in the 1930s, 1940s, and 1950s. Over the last forty years, with the spread of development and urbanization along the coast of California, the cove has become an even more popular place to paint. It is one of the few remaining areas of unspoiled splendor easily accessed from most of Southern California.

This is due in great part to the efforts of the Crystal Cove Conservancy and to the untiring work of Laura Davick, her associates, and the California State Parks system, who uphold the cove's matchless distinction. It is thanks to them that Crystal Cove will remain truly a breathtaking bit of Eden.

Jean Stern
Executive Director
The Irvine Museum Collection
at the University of California, Irvine

Foreword

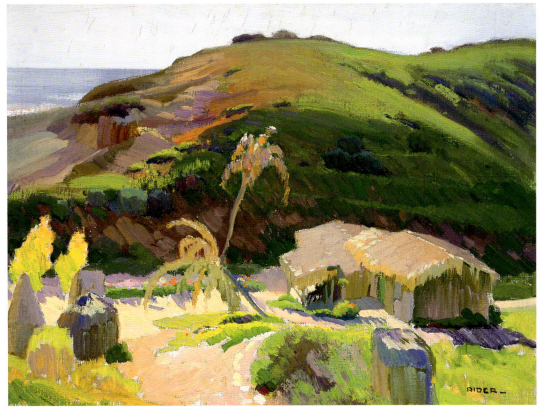

TOP:
Crystal Cove
by William Wendt
(oil on canvas, 28 x 36, 1912).

BOTTOM:
Near Laguna
by Arthur G. Rider's
(oil on canvas, 16 x 21, c. 1928).

Introduction

On an August evening sometime in the mid-1950s, as another perfect Southern California day drew down to darkness, a small sailboat on its way home to the Newport Beach harbor skated too close to shore and found itself trapped in the surf. The sailors were starting to panic when a group of browned and burly men on the shore spotted them and swam out through the black water to help beach the boat. As they landed, the smell of roasting meat wafted over from what looked to be a village of thatched huts set amongst palm trees and tropical growth. On the beach, a group of natives sat around a bonfire, drinking and singing. Behind this cozy enclave rose empty hills glowing golden in the day's last light; there was no other sign of human habitation. "My God," one of the sailors gasped. "Where *are* we? How far did we drift?"

They had strayed just a mile and a half. They'd landed not on some South Pacific island but on the rustic shores of Crystal Cove, California, beloved retreat of vacationing American families. Like many old, perhaps apocryphal, stories about the cove, this one reveals an essential truth about the place: to those who summered there, the life was ideal; to passersby, it seemed impossibly exotic, a tropical fantasia, a mirage. It is a tale from one of California's golden ages, when automobile motoring had opened up new vistas and beach colonies sprang up along the coast from Malibu to San Diego. A time when it was legal to dive for abalone—and there were still abalone left to dive for. When the hills beyond the beach were thick with coyote bush and toyon and sage.

It's hard now to recall what Orange County looked like then, when its rolling plains held little besides yellow pastures and orange groves. A drive down the Pacific Coast Highway today reveals mile after mile of housing developments, shopping malls, time-share condos, and golf courses. And yet, remarkably, Crystal Cove—a small settlement of timeworn cottages tucked into an otherwise undeveloped three-mile stretch of beach—remains frozen in time.

LEFT:
The boardwalk to the north end of the beach disappears behind cottage 12.

BELOW:
Bathing beauties of the cove, 1940s.

BOTTOM:
Luau party on the beach, 1960.

There's a distinct feeling of time travel that accompanies any visit to the cove. The turnoff from the Pacific Coast Highway quickly drops down to a one-lane road snaking under towering eucalyptus trees and through embankments overgrown with nasturtiums. The roar of highway traffic gives way to the slow, rhythmic build and crash of waves. The smell of Old California reaches up from the past: the winelike ferment of warm ice plant and eucalyptus, the velvety dust of crumbling road, and the tang of drying seaweed—all wrapped in a fine mesh of ocean salt. The cottages, too, look much as they ever have, an appealingly haphazard collection of architectural odds and ends nestled in so cozily that they seem to have grown here, twining along the bluffs with the bougainvillea and morning glory.

What is this oasis in time, and how did it remain untouched while the rest of the region evolved into a modern suburban landscape? The cove's origins date back to the early 1920s and an unusual agreement between a

Introduction

powerful landowner and a handful of California families: rancher James Irvine Jr., who owned the cove, allowed people to camp on an unused slip of his vast property and eventually construct simple vacation cabins there, but he retained ownership of the land under them. A naturalist, Irvine preferred to leave much of his land in an untamed state, and through the years not much changed here. But despite its uniqueness and isolation, the cove acted as a microcosm of California history. It was a set for Hollywood filmmakers during the silent-film boom, a drop-off spot for Prohibition-era rumrunners, a destination for motorists during the early auto-touring movement, a staging ground for postwar tiki parties and luaus, and a continual source of inspiration for nearby Laguna's famed art community. Through it all, however, the place never seemed to change. Without the right to sell or develop the land, the residents—and their houses—were locked in time, and Crystal Cove remained a simple beach colony while nearby coastal development skyrocketed.

LEFT:
Los Trancos Creek passing between cottages on its way to the ocean.

BELOW:
Crystal Quiet by Michael Obermeyer (oil on canvas, 12 x 16, 2002).

With Irvine's death came a decision about the future of this last remaining undeveloped piece of Orange County coastline. Luckily his vision prevailed, and in 1979 the Irvine Company sold the cove, and nearly three thousand acres surrounding it, to the California Department of Parks and Recreation for the formation of Crystal Cove State Park. In order to make the cove a true public park accessible to all Californians, the longtime residents eventually moved out. Today the cottages continue to proffer their funky charm as research facilities, educational and interpretive centers, and overnight vacation rentals for park visitors.

Crystal Cove has always been an expression of individuality, so any history of it must celebrate the people who made it a place like no other: its early amateur architects, the activists who worked to protect it, the families who maintained its history over multiple generations, and the larger-than-life personalities who enlivened day-to-day activity on the beach. Though the members of this community are no longer gathered in residence here, their legacy, and their spirit, is palpable. No matter how much the cove changes, in some essential way it always stays the same; its singular atmosphere is inherent and cannot be lost. If places, like people, can be said to have natural genius, then Crystal Cove is a savant. It is overgrown to perfection, both casual and glamorous, welcoming and discreet—all without ever seeming to try. Park visitors today are still amazed at what they have stumbled upon. They sense what enchanted those rescued sailors, the spirit of this unlikely paradise on the sand.

The porch outside Cottage #6.

Introduction

Shallow Water, Soft Breeze by John Cosby
(oil on linen, 42 x 60, 2003).

Chapter 1

Unspoiled Vistas

THE COVE BEFORE 1917

> We traveled through the rancho [San Joaquin], the property of James Irvine, a distance of nearly twelve miles, during which we saw no house nor found any improvement.
>
> — *Santa Ana Herald*, December 31, 1881 —

In March of 1994,

construction workers digging a storm drain for a new entrance road to Crystal Cove State Park stopped what they were doing. They had struck a buried layer of mussel shells, crab claws, and sardine and shark bones near the mouth of Los Trancos Creek, five hundred feet from the ocean. The twelve-foot-deep stratum of ancient food debris was an Indian midden, a sort of garbage pile where migratory Native Americans had collected their food waste before moving on to another camp. Other middens had been discovered farther upstream, on the slopes of the San Joaquin Hills, but this was the most intact. What it revealed was telling: even four thousand years ago, local families had camped at the slight dip in the coastal bluff where Los Trancos winds its way down from the hills and empties into the sea.

An archaeological study of the debris indicated that it was seasonal: this was the site of a summer fishing camp. Much as twentieth-century families had packed up their belongings and traveled each May to Crystal Cove, an extended clan of ancient Native Americans had spent the warmer months there as well. Like their latter-day counterparts, the Indians would have considered this the easy time of year: they spent days on the beach gathering mussels from the rocks, built and launched fishing boats, and lit campfires at night, eating well on their favorite foods. Signs also indicated that the Indians at this and other nearby summer camps had suddenly left the area some thirty-seven hundred years ago, much as Crystal Cove's modern community would abruptly decamp in 2001.

What made the Indians leave remains a mystery, but there has been no other sign of habitation at the cove until the early twentieth century. The surrounding territory was claimed by Spanish explorers in the sixteenth century, fell within the holdings of Mission San Juan Capistrano, founded in 1776, and later went to Jose Andres Sepulveda, scion of a wealthy Spanish family that helped found Los Angeles, in a Mexican land grant. But there is no evidence that any of these owners ever set sight on this tiny and remote sliver of their vast property. Few roads were built, and most of the area—including Crystal Cove—remained a secluded wilderness.

When floods and a series of droughts devastated the Mexican ranchos of Southern California, American livestock owners seized the opportunity to pick up large tracts of land cheaply. In 1864, heavily in debt, Sepulveda sold all forty-eight thousand acres of his Rancho San Joaquin to the sheep-ranching firm of Flint, Bixby, and Irvine for $18,000. Additional acquisitions brought the company's holdings to nearly one hundred and fifteen thousand acres. A local newspaper called it "about the most remarkable transaction in real estate ever known in this section." When financial reversals forced Thomas and Benjamin Flint and Llewellyn Bixby to sell their interests, the remaining partner, real estate investor James Irvine, became sole owner of the eight-mile-long, twenty-two-mile-wide property that would later be known as the Irvine Ranch.

A view of the beach from the bluff.

PREVIOUS SPREAD:
A rock outcropping north of Crystal Cove.

Crystal Cove Cottages

The beach at sunset.

Unspoiled Vistas The Cove before 1917

The first tide pools south of the cottages.

While other landowners favored subdividing and development, Irvine stubbornly followed an agrarian model. Locals contended that his wild and underutilized acres were standing in the way of progress, preventing improvements such as orderly street grids and productive farm parcels. Irvine also obstructed the railroads, refusing to let them build across his land and preventing the degree of development they spurred elsewhere.

When Irvine died in 1886, his son, James Irvine Jr., known as "JI," inherited the ranch. In June 1894 JI incorporated his inheritance as the Irvine Company. Around this time the southernmost cities of Los Angeles County won the right to establish a local county seat and formed Orange County. The Irvine Ranch occupied between a quarter and a third of the new county's area.

Because JI shared his father's conservation principles, the Irvine Ranch continued to maintain a rural presence while economic development cropped up around it. Another pioneer developer of the area, Henry Huntington, might have been JI's polar opposite. He built the electric Red Car line to his holdings in Newport Beach and Balboa in 1905—opening seaside resorts to a growing urban population in the pre-auto days—and constructed palatial bathhouses and beach clubs. The Irvines, meanwhile, held onto the majority of their vast property, significantly slowing down the overall pace of development in Orange County. Some parts of the ranch were farmed, but the area that is now Crystal Cove State Park was most likely used for grazing until the late 1920s.

Property in those days was primarily valued for what a landowner could graze or grow on it, and sandy coastal beaches—which might be million-dollar properties today—had negligible monetary worth. The Irvines spent leisure time at a spot they called the "Family Cove," but no other use was made of the ranch's ocean

beaches. It didn't seem to bother JI, then, that locals were starting to explore another little inlet at the mouth of a small creek on his land.

It is not known who came first to Crystal Cove, but three main groups took an interest in the area at the time: Irvine employees and sharecroppers looking to relax, landscape painters seeking outdoor vistas for their canvases, and Hollywood filmmakers in need of rustic locations for movies set in exotic locales.

The earliest known image of Crystal Cove is a painting by William Wendt (1865–1946) dated 1912. A community of artists based in Laguna frequently traveled the region by horseback and camped in the wilderness for a few days at a time, setting up their easels outdoors, a method known as "plein air painting." When Irvine sold a small development called Emerald Bay in 1906, a dirt road was constructed from there to Corona del Mar, passing Crystal Cove, but since it did not continue through to other towns, few people took it. Wendt is the only recorded visitor to the cove before 1916, when the dirt road was extended south to Laguna and traffic began passing through sporadically. The recent invention of the automobile had spurred interest in travel and recreation, and the road, though rugged, was one of many scenic byways popularized during that era.

By the late teens Crystal Cove had regular visitors: painters came from Laguna and sightseers from Corona del Mar. Road builders did not initially grade a turnoff at the cove, but Los Trancos Creek is dry in the summer, so early visitors could drive right down the creek bed, hiking in farther to reach this deserted stretch of beach. Irvine allowed his workers to camp overnight at the beach, and soon their friends and families were joining them. Technically these visitors were trespassing on Irvine property, but JI had long wanted this area of the coastline to be public, and eventually he legitimized the deal by charging campers an overnight fee. Meanwhile, early filmmakers were renting boats at Newport Harbor and scouting the shores for interesting locations. When they saw the shallow lagoon that Los Trancos Creek formed as it joined the Pacific, they thought the spot looked a bit like a tropical island. Crystal Cove had begun to work its magic on Californians of all kinds.

PREVIOUS SPREAD:
An untitled 1923 painting by Jack Wilkinson Smith (oil on canvas, 52 x 70), believed to be inspired by the view from Reef Point at Crystal Cove.

Unspoiled Vistas   The Cove before 1917

William Wendt's 1912 painting *Crystal Cove*
(oil on canvas, 28 x 36)
is the earliest recorded image of the cove.

Crystal Cove Cottages

Wendt's *The Old Coast Road* (oil on canvas, 30 x 37, 1916)
shows the dirt road through Laguna, looking north toward Crystal Cove,
as it was in the early 1900s.

TOP RIGHT:
Iridescent Evening by Frank Cuprien
(oil on board, 15 x 18, 1925).

BOTTOM RIGHT:
Barse Miller's *Road to Capistrano*
(watercolor, 12 3/4 x 18 1/8, c. 1930) shows
the section of the Old Coast Road that
passed Crystal Cove.

29

Plein Air Painters in Laguna Beach and Crystal Cove

By Meriam Braselle

Artist Liaison, Laguna Plein Air Painters Association

The art of painting *en plein air*, or outdoors, started nearly 150 years ago in France with the advent of impressionism. In the United States, impressionist-style painting began in the late nineteenth century, when colonies of plein air artists formed around the country. One of the more famous sprang up in Laguna Beach, where the combination of moderate climate and natural beauty attracted European as well as American artists—including Edgar Payne, William Wendt, Frank Cuprien, Joseph Kleitsch, Jack Wilkinson Smith, and Anna Hills—in the early 1900s. The artists were steeped in traditional training from such respected institutions as the School of the Art Institute of Chicago, the Art Students League in New York, the Pennsylvania Academy of the Fine Arts, and L'Ecole des Beaux-Arts and Academie Julian, both in Paris. Many were members of the California Art Club, founded in 1909.

Laguna Beach quickly became known as an art colony and cultural oasis. In 1918, under the leadership of Edgar Payne, a small group of artists founded the Laguna Beach Art Association. One of the objectives of the association was "to advance the knowledge [of] and interest in art and to create a spirit of cooperation and fellowship between painter and public." Not only did these artists have a direct influence on the economy of Laguna Beach by attracting tourists, art collectors, and students to the area, they were also instrumental in forming the infrastructure of the community. Anna Hills (1882–1930), who was president of the association for several terms during the 1920s, was one of the area's first environmentalists, organizing tree plantings along Laguna Canyon Road. She also helped found the Laguna Beach Fire Department, developed art programs in the public schools, and was involved in the Laguna Presbyterian Church, where several of her paintings still hang.

The early impressionist painters felt a need and responsibility to document the landscape for the joy and education of future generations. In the days when photography was still a nascent art form, it was their work that captured the undiscovered coast and helped draw Americans west. We can thank these painters for providing some of the first visual documentation of Orange County's untamed, pristine coastline, with its secluded coves, vertical bluffs, and white sand beaches—including Crystal Cove. Although the dirt road leading north from Laguna Beach across the Irvine Ranch was private, it did allow for limited access to the many sunlit bluffs and beaches, where one could paint in solitude for days. The painters talked of finding solitude in their total immersion in the natural setting; for them it evoked a feeling of overwhelming exhilaration and closeness to God, a "sense of spirit" that they associated specifically with these remote locations.

Plein Air Painters in Laguna Beach and Crystal Cove

TOP:
Eternal Surge by Edgar Payne (oil on canvas, 34 x 45, c. 1921).

BOTTOM:
Beach Shack Study by Jacobus Baas (oil on canvas, 11 x 14, 2000).

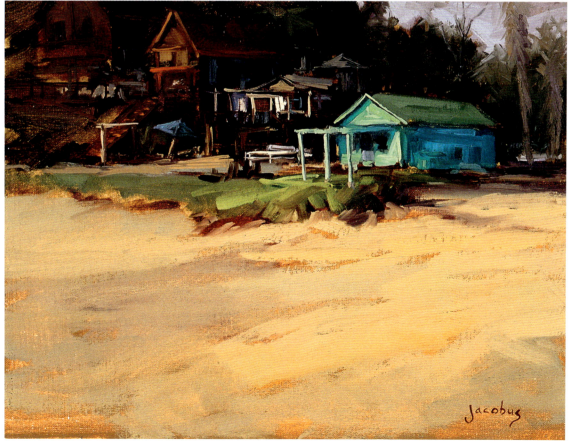

Crystal Cove Cottages

High Tide, Laguna Beach by Anna Hills (oil on canvas, 20 x 30, 1914).

TOP RIGHT:
Anna Hills painting outdoors, 1913.

RIGHT:
Frank Cuprien in Laguna Beach, 1935.

Crystal Cove Cottages

RIGHT:
Laguna Beach painting class, 1933.

FAR RIGHT:
An untitled painting of the cove by Roger Kuntz (oil on canvas, 30 x 40, c.1970).

BOTTOM RIGHT:
Arthur G. Rider's *Near Laguna* (oil on canvas, 16 x 21, c. 1928). Rider came to the cove as a set painter for MGM Studios.

As Crystal Cove's architecture evolved, painters documented its development. Plein air artist Arthur Rider's (1886–1975) painting *Near Laguna*, with its palm-thatched structure, depicts the first cottage built at the entry to Crystal Cove. Rider—who had studied painting in Chicago, Paris, and Valencia, Spain—was also a sought-after set painter for Twentieth Century Fox and Metro-Goldwyn-Mayer studios, and first came to the cove on a film assignment.

Artists who lived or stayed at Crystal Cove were many. One of the most famous was Roger Kuntz (1926–1975), a member of the Claremont Group of painters—professors and graduates of Pomona College, Scripps College, and the Claremont Graduate School. Each summer for many years, Kuntz and his family spent a month in the Kortlander family's cottage at Crystal Cove, where he would set up an outdoor studio in the front yard. Other artists who lived and worked at the cove included Jim Fuller; Douglas McClellan; Bonnie Gregory; Vivian Falzetti; Alice Powell, whose studio behind Cottage #32 included a kiln for firing her painted porcelains; and Roger Armstrong, former director of what is now Laguna Art Museum.

In a sense, many of the residents of Crystal Cove had artistic abilities. The architectural elements of each cottage were enhanced by the addition of handmade porches, stairways, windows, shutters, and awnings, some of which had such a whimsical character that the cottages seemed to come to life. As the architecture evolved, so did the collection of artifacts and artwork, weaving the cultural fabric of generations.

With the advent of modernism, the traditional plein air style of painting declined in popularity. However, many artists continued to employ its techniques, finding that it remained the ideal method for painting realistic landscapes and seascapes. In the 1970s, art historians began to write about the history of impressionist painting in California, bringing plein air painting back into the public consciousness. Over the next three decades a resurgence in plein air techniques led painters around the country to organize new groups, such as the Laguna Plein Air Painters Association (LPAPA) in Laguna Beach. In the summer of 1999, in collaboration with Laguna Art Museum, LPAPA invited top artists from around the country to a plein air painting competition. The invitational was so successful that it has become a much-anticipated annual event.

The competition also raised considerable funds for the museum, continuing the landscape painters' tradition of supporting their community and its natural resources. Inspired by the California Art Club, which had helped save historic buildings in Los Angeles's Chinatown and Pasadena's Craftsman neighborhoods, the artists of LPAPA dedicated their efforts to the preservation of Crystal Cove. Today *plein air* painters continue to document the area, raising public awareness of the cove. The Park Interpretive Store also serves as a local art gallery, and the Crystal Cove Conservancy offers *plein air* painting classes, ensuring that the 100-year-long tradition of *plein air* painting lives on at the cove. But more important, these activities integrate artists into the community, reinforcing the importance of their perspective to the continued evolution of the cove. The park's programs provide an opportunity for intellectual exchange between painters, biologists, writers, filmmakers, teachers, and students. Contemporary artists contribute not just their talent but also the inspiration that comes from the intimate experience of creating in a natural environment—the same sense of spirit that the early plein air painters found at Crystal Cove.

Crystal Cove Cottages

Crystal Cove Cottage by Cynthia Britain
(oil on canvas, 18 x 24, 1998).

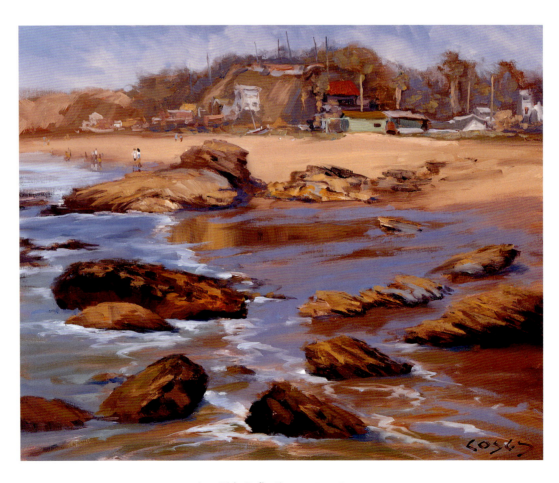

Low Tide Reflections by John Cosby
(oil on linen, 20 x 24, 2001).

The Green Mantle by Jeffrey C. Horn
(oil on canvas, 18 x 24, 2001).

Crystal Cove Cottages

Day at the Beach by Roger Kuntz
(oil on canvas, 18 x 24, c. 1970).

Crystal Cove State Park by Saim Caglayan
(oil on canvas, 11 x 14, 2001).

Crystal Cove by Ken Auster
(oil on canvas, 11 x 14, 2001).

Crystal Cove Cottages

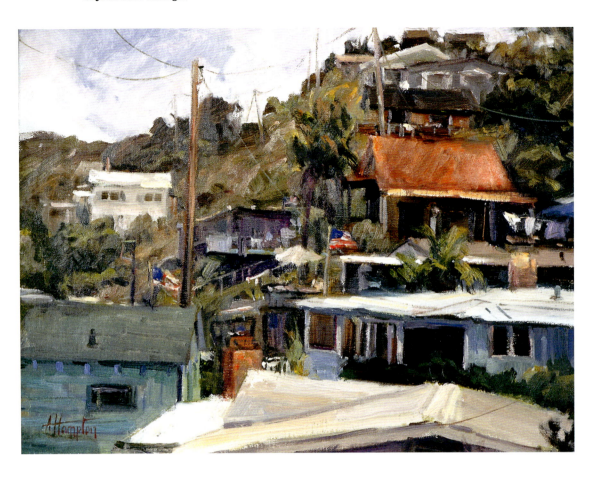

ABOVE:
A Remembered Community
by Anita Hampton
(oil on linen, 14 x 18, 2001).

RIGHT:
Off the Edge
by Jeffrey C. Horn
(oil on canvas,
16 x 20, 2002).

Plein Air Painters in Laguna Beach and Crystal Cove

Crystal Cove by Calvin Liang
(oil on canvas, 6 x 8, 2001).

Cottage #00

The Office

One of the first cottages you come across upon entering Crystal Cove is also the first permanent structure to be built here, in 1925. That year, James Irvine Jr. hired the cove's first manager, E. Roy Davidson, a Hollywood technical director, to oversee campsite rentals and movie shoots. Roy and his friend Merrill Wood built the one-room office; subsequent managers added living quarters in the back, turned the main room into a living room, and moved business activities to a glassed-in front porch. The cottage's quirks exemplified cove architecture; the bedrooms, for example, were attached but could be accessed only from exterior stairs, as there were no interior hallways. Gone is the makeshift security system that manager Laura McMenomy rigged up in the 1950s, consisting of an airport landing light and loudspeaker atop the roof. (If intruders tried to breach the entrance gate late at night, Laura could flood the area with light and broadcast her scoldings over the loudspeaker.) Extant original architectural details of this cottage include shiplap siding, wooden sash and casement windows, French doors, a round call bell in the kitchen, and a mail slot outside the office door, which cove residents and campers used to pay their rent to the Irvine Company. Today the old office serves as the Visitor Center for the Crystal Cove Historic District.

TOP RIGHT:
Crystal Cove entrance road and office, 1930s.

RIGHT:
The office as the residence of Danny and Natalie Falzetti, 2001.

LEFT:
The office in 1979.

Crystal Cove Cottages

Laura McMenomy and her son, Bob (left), and nephew Tom Holmes outside the office. Laura and Bob were the cove's managers from 1954 to 1972.

Cottage #00

BELOW:
Road to the Sea by Meriam Braselle
(oil on canvas, 11 x 14, 2000).

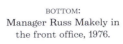

BOTTOM:
Manager Russ Makely in
the front office, 1976.

45

Cottage #2

The Davick Cottage

The cove's third cottage started out as a movie set. It was built in 1926 by brothers-in-law Russell Paull and Lowell Bailey, Huntington Beach oilfield workers who earned extra money doing construction in the area. After filming was done, their families used the cottage on weekends, later selling it to four bank tellers from Azusa—Elsie Bantley, Margaret Orndorf, Ruth Hepner, and Dorothy Sproul—who shared it as a vacation house. When the women had a new house built next door, they sold Cottage #2 to Joseph Sheeder, a tenter who worked in Hollywood and had first visited the cove during a film shoot. He added a front porch and an indoor bathroom, and in the late 1940s he gave the cottage to his daughter, Virginia, as a wedding present.

The one-room cottage stayed relatively unchanged until 1961, when tent campers Bob and Peggy Davick took over the lease. Over the years Bob, an engineer, enclosed the patio and added a new deck, two bedrooms, and an office. Rooms were built from a combination of standard construction materials and flotsam found on the beach: the deck, for example, once had seating made from boat hatch covers. Whenever he completed a major addition, Bob scavenged driftwood from the beach to cover the seams. In later years his daughter Laura Davick crafted rockwork on the front of the house with stones, shells, and beach glass. Inside the cottage today hangs a shell collage made by Mabel Webb, Peggy's mother. The cottage is now available to park visitors for overnight rental and is known as the Shell Shack.

LEFT:
Mailbox decor.

BOTTOM LEFT:
The Davick children, Laura, Stephen, and Susan, on the porch with shell mobiles, 1964.

TOP RIGHT:
Laura's open-air patio bedroom offered the best view in the house.

CENTER RIGHT:
Laura Davick on the deck her father built, 2001.

NEAR RIGHT:
Cottage #2 as film set, 1926.

FAR RIGHT:
Palm fronds still required, 1938.

Chapter 2

Silent Films and Palm Fronds

1917 to 1940

On the Coast Highway between Balboa and Laguna is a bathing resort that has the atmosphere of a South Sea atoll. Touring along the highway recently, a party from the Paige Company of Southern California in a Paige 6-65 cabriolet, saw thatched huts and long-fronded palms marking the beach of Crystal Cove. You're wrong—this is not Waikiki Beach!

— *Los Angeles Examiner*, August 14, 1927 —

It was Crystal Cove's good fortune to lie just between Balboa and Laguna, one a vibrant social scene of bath pavilions and beach clubs, the other a sleepy outpost of rusticating artists who were most at home gazing out upon unpopulated vistas. To those who were lucky enough to discover it, the cove was a happy medium. It was only a two-hour drive from the Los Angeles area, but upon arrival the sense of isolation was complete: no crowds, no expenses, no need to dress for dinner.

There was also no gas, no electricity, and no running water. The cove attracted a more rugged breed of vacationer, one who preferred a tent and a camp stove to a hotel room and a restaurant—whether by dint of personal philosophy or personal finances. It was a long trip by Model T, and at the end of it there was still a short hike to the beach.

The cove's location may have been most ideal for Hollywood moviemakers, who were filming silent black-and-white pictures such as *Treasure Island* there as early as 1917. Audiences of the time favored stories of shipwrecks and tropical islands, but short production times and low budgets kept directors on a tight leash; the trick was to re-create Polynesia in Southern California. The stretch of beach where the cove lay was unspoiled by houses, power lines, piers, and boats—yet still within driving distance of civilization. At Crystal Cove, a crew could spend the day filming on what looked to be a remote island, then repair to Newport or Balboa for dinner and drinks. To create a tropical setting for movies like *The Sea Wolf*, *Stormswept*, *Sadie Thompson*, and *Half a Bride*—featuring such stars as Gloria Swanson, Lionel Barrymore, and Gary Cooper—film crews built small thatched huts and trucked palm trees down from Los Angeles nurseries. The trees thrived in the coastal climate and became part of the ambiance; almost every palm tree at the cove today was planted by early filmmakers. Some of the "huts" remained as well and eventually took on lives of their own as vacation rentals.

With this much activity at the cove, JI needed someone to oversee things. The earliest official managers at the cove were E. Roy Davidson, a technical director for film producers, and his wife, Donna. But their friends Merrill and Beth Wood were also involved in running the camping concession and building early structures. In fact it was Beth, an avid swimmer, who named the cove. According to the Woods' son Ron, "The water in those days was so clear that you could see down right to the sand. It was crystal clear, and that's where she came up with the name Crystal Cove." Merrill, a general contractor, was responsible for much of the cove's early infrastructure. "My dad made the road that goes down to the

PREVIOUS SPREAD:
Thatched huts and palm trees on the beach, early 1920s.

Early tenting was primitive: no gas, no electricity, no running water.

A movie set at the mouth of Los Trancos Creek.

Silent Films and Palm Fronds 1917 to 1940

beach," Ron said. "He carved it out with a couple of Mexicans, using pick and shovel and wheelbarrows." Merrill and Roy also built a small office (the first permanent structure at the cove) in 1925. From this base of operations they ran the cove, as additional cabins sprang up and the number of visitors started to grow.

Now California had people living in it—3.5 million, in fact—and the people had cars. They also had jobs and housework and other sources of stress, and therefore a reason to get in their cars and drive as far as they could go. But improved roads didn't take them very far, so automobile clubs began pressuring the state legislature to build highways and increase access to the beaches along the Orange County coast. The growing leagues of day-trippers and auto campers got what they wanted in the Pacific Coast Highway, the most famous scenic route in California, if not the world. The road featured state-of-the-art construction, and its opening was welcomed with all the pomp of a presidential visit. On October 9, 1926, a parade of decorated automobiles proceeded from Long Beach to Laguna Beach, where Mary Pickford and Douglas Fairbanks ceremonially forged the last link in a chain of flowers held by bathing beauties from each of the coastal communities.

With the highway complete, many more people began to discover the charm of the wild, uninhabited Orange County coast. No longer the well-kept secret of Hollywood insiders and Irvine Ranch employees, the cove was now open for the stumbling upon—and in fact that's exactly how many longtime cove residents first came here. Word spread through neighborhoods and workplaces, and soon the beach was lined with camping families, their kerosene lanterns and bonfires flickering against the great dark backdrop of Irvine's undeveloped land like the torches of a wilderness outpost. During the day they swam and fished in the surf, took long, restorative walks, and collected shells from the tide pools. The ones who fell in love with this simple routine returned year after year, pitching their tents in the same spot each summer. Families gradually stayed longer and longer, some eventually spending the entire summer, from the last day of one school year to the first day of the next.

Longer stays required sturdier and more habitable accommodations, and the movie-set huts gave the campers some ideas. But the incident that set genuine property improvement in motion was something far more random. It's no coincidence that the first cabins built

Donna Davidson (left) and Beth Wood, wives of the cove's first managers, with Beth's son Jerry. When studios filmed at the cove, crews left the sets—including tropical plants—behind, turning the coastal scrub landscape into a miniature jungle.

by campers went up in 1927, the year the *Esther Buhne*, a 287-foot schooner, wrecked on Balboa Point. "A lot of lumber came into the cove and people started to build cottages where they had been building their tents," said Bud Carter, whose family bought Cottage #7 in the 1930s. "They just built—no permits or plans." It's rumored that the boat was a lumber schooner, but more likely it was just a large vessel whose washed-up remains provided enough teak to build several small one-room cabins. (An excellent example of teak single-wall construction is the dark, woody interior of Cottage #8, the least altered of the original cabins.)

There was no way to reach these new structures except to trudge across the sand, so the campers used some of the teak to build a boardwalk.

In 1928 Roy Davidson sublet the cove to Estella and Gustave Paull, who took over running the camping concession and a small sandwich stand on the beach. Some of the most vivid early impressions of the cove on record come from the Paulls' son John, who was twelve years old when his family arrived. John recalled movie actors having parties on the beach after the day's filming was done. "In the evening they all got to boozing it up," he said. "They would hold up dimes between their fingers and let me shoot at them with my BB gun. I always made a lot of sore fingers." John also recalled the 1920s as an active time for illicit offshore activities—this was, after all, the era of Prohibition, and the cove was a conveniently hidden spot only four miles from Laguna and one mile from Corona del Mar. Liquor boats painted black moored just off the cove while rumrunners smuggled their cargo ashore. "Somebody would come across the fields from Coast Highway in a truck, and they would unload the whiskey and take it off in the truck," John remembered. "They would put it into a big canvas and lower it over the side [of the boat] if they figured the Coast Guard was after them." The rumrunners and their activities sparked a mixture of fear and excitement in the residents. Several remember being terrified to see cars pulling up next to the cottages late at night and signaling to the boats with their headlights. Others fondly recall poking long sticks deep into the drifted sand and sometimes finding mislaid cases of booze buried by the tide. According

ABOVE:
Crystal Cove as filmmaking colony.

to Ron Wood, one year word got out that surf fishermen were finding bottles rolling in the waves, and the cove enjoyed a sudden surge in popularity.

John Paull also told of playing with children from across the highway, sons of the Japanese American sharecroppers who made a living off of Irvine's hilly, rugged coastal shelf. These were truck farmers who grew fruits and vegetables to sell in fresh markets and roadside stands. The hills made irrigation difficult, so the farmers had to rely on the natural sluice of rainfall. Luckily the coastal region was also free of frost, which made it ideal for growing the popular Kentucky Wonder Bean, or string bean. The farmers thrived and word of their success brought others to the area. Twelve Japanese families were living at this edge of the ranch by the 1930s, selling vegetables at roadside stands and sometimes fishing for octopus down at the cove. They built a schoolhouse where, on Saturdays, their children studied Japanese and practiced traditional martial arts.

The cove was a democratic establishment, and its residents made up a fairly heterogeneous neighborhood for the time. The Parkers, of Cottage #13, were in

Bud Carter and his mother, Pearl, in front of cottage 7.
His father, Alfred, painted the "Pearl Harbor" sign hanging to the right.
He took it down after the real Pearl Harbor was attacked.

pest control, while their neighbor, Edith Henning, was a secretary for the legendary movie makeup artist Max Factor (and rumored to be his girlfriend). Cecil Payne, a structural engineer who had designed dams in Ecuador and Peru, built Cottage #11 for his wife, an Irish immigrant called Biddy. Some enterprising college boys from Pasadena were said to have started Cottage #18, up on the bluff. Dr. Paul Van Degrift built Cottage #28 for his family when he was in medical school.

In 1930 a clan of former circus performers joined this mix when the Hoey family took over the lease of the cove from Roy Davidson. The country was in

ABOVE:
Manager George Hoey (far left) and neighbors outside an early incarnation of the store, c. 1930.

RIGHT:
The palm-thatched store surrounded by tents, early 1930s.

an economic depression, but little was required in order to live the good life on the beach: entertainment was free, cooking and clothing were casual at best, building materials were scavenged, and furnishings were often castoffs from family and friends. Some of the cottages became permanent residences, suggesting that financial need played a role in their construction, but most were built for recreation. In both cases frugality and ingenuity were imperative. Unless campers wanted to wait for another shipwreck, getting materials to the cove required creative vision. The Miller family laid the foundation for Cottage #12 out of telephone poles that they floated up from San Diego, pulled by a boat. Their front windows were scavenged from the Riverside Hotel when it underwent restoration, and a discarded bathroom sink came from the Hotel del Coronado, in San Diego. "A lot of the wood just came off the beach," said George Fuller Jr., whose father built Cottage #9. "No building codes—they just went down to the beach or the wrecking yard, brought stuff in, and put it up." Most of the cabins were board-and-batten single-wall construction with no insulation. "You could see the light coming between the boards," George added. "It was like being outdoors." Each cabin

Crystal Cove Cottages

FAR LEFT, TOP:
George Fuller Jr. and his parents, George Sr. and Sylvia.

FAR LEFT, BOTTOM:
George Fuller Jr. playing on the beach, 1929.

TOP LEFT:
George Fuller Sr. and Jr., 1930.

BOTTOM LEFT:
Bathing suits of the day—Marcelle Sloane of cottage 10 (right) with a neighbor, 1933.

TOP:
The Sheeder family of cottage 2 with friends, 1930. Joe is in the plaid shirt on the right, next to his wife, Kathleen, who holds their daughter Virginia on her lap.

TOP RIGHT:
Beth and Merrill Wood with their son Jerry.

CENTER RIGHT:
The cove was known for its surf fishing.

BOTTOM RIGHT:
Tent campers Guy and Mabel Webb and their son, Tom, unpacking for the summer, 1937.

A color postcard from the 1930s advertises an idealized version of Crystal Cove.

had an outhouse, and potbellied stoves provided heat.

When electricity came to the cove in the 1930s it was knob-and-tube style: bare wires strung through small insulated knobs mounted on interior ceilings and walls. The arrival of gas a few years later led to another amenity: addresses. Cottages #1 through #9 appear to have been numbered in the order in which they were built; from #10 on they were numbered according to when they received their gas hookup. Thus, #12 is next to #3, and #14 sits between #17 and #21. The one consistency among the cottages was their palm-frond roofs, which the Hoeys required: it attracted filmmakers, who then paid a fee for shooting privileges.

One sign of the Depression and its toll elsewhere in the country was the Okies who had fled to California from the dust bowl states, sometimes stopping at the cove for a rest. "A progression of old cars pulled into parking places and seemingly large families would move out onto the sand," Phyllis Parker Lowe, of Cottage #13, recalled. "Slender youngsters shed their shirts and pounced into the waves, clad in their Levi's, while their mothers hiked up their farm dresses and just waded in. From what we learned, and from the regularity of the event, we could not fault their joy in the ocean, nor their overdressed strangeness."

The years just before the start of World War II were some of the happiest at the cove. According to Bud Carter, "It was a grand time to be fifteen, sixteen, seventeen years old with a cottage at Crystal Cove. The tenters would come, and along with some of them came their daughters: campfires every night, dancing in front of the store. We would sometimes go to the Rendezvous Ballroom in Balboa for an evening of dancing to one of the big bands like Claude Thornhill or Stan Kenton."

By the late 1930s there were at least forty-five cottages at the cove, possibly more. James Irvine's sleepy tenting ground was starting to take on the character of a small village. Over the years the Irvine Company had sold off portions of coastline to settle property-tax debts, and rumors were always circulating that Crystal Cove would be next. JI was grooming his son, James III, to take over the ranch, and in 1931 he sent the younger Irvine to strike a deal with the Federal Board of Tax Appeals that would clear some Irvine Ranch tax debts in exchange for the stretch of coastline from Corona del Mar to Crystal Cove, which was to become a national park. Though the tax board agreed to the terms, James III became ill with tuberculosis and was unable to see them through. He died four years later, at the age of forty-two. The tax bill was eventually resolved by payment, and the land remained part of the Irvine Ranch.

JI had expected his eldest son to succeed him and manage the ranch. Now

Easter vacation, 1942.

Crystal Cove Cottages

An aerial photo taken from very high shows the Japanese sharecroppers' terrace farms and homes.

robbed of that possibility, he created a charitable foundation to take control of the ranch upon his death. Whether this had any immediate impact on the cove is unknown, but in late 1939 the Irvine Company did issue a notice to the residents of Crystal Cove along with their annual lease, which stated that beginning January 1, 1940, all leases would be ten-year agreements (replacing the year-to-year leases the Irvine Company had previously issued). Any buildings on the property would become "part and parcel of the land and belong to the Lessor (the Irvine Company)." Tenants could sign the ten-year lease and forgo ownership rights to their cottages, or they could move them to another location. With no legal claim to the land they had built on, the tenants had no choice but to comply. A few did haul their cottages off to other addresses; at least one can now be found in Laguna Beach. The other families, smitten with the idyllic site and its rugged, romantic lifestyle, resolved to stay, homeowners or not. They would do whatever they could to remain "coveites" for as long as possible.

Chubby Old Palm by Carole Cooke (oil on linen, 12 x 10, 1999). Almost every palm tree at the cove today was planted by early filmmakers.

Cottage #13

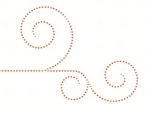

The Beaches Cottage

Perhaps the most iconic cove structure is the "Beaches" cottage, so named because it appeared in the 1988 Bette Midler film. The farthest south of all the cottages, it is set off a little from the others, perched below a bluff, with the cove's picturesque tide pools jutting into the sea just in front of it. Generations of photographers and painters have found that, shown from the right angle, #13 can look as though it is the only house on the beach.

But the dark-brown shingled two-story had humble beginnings. The six couples who built it first came to the cove as campers in the late 1920s. The families were happy in their tents but wanted a sand-free place to cook and eat, so they built a ten-by-twelve-foot room with a small porch, wooden floors set on concrete posts, and walls that were four feet high. Screens made up the top half of the walls, and the roof was made of canvas acquired from the fumigation business that two of the families owned. They built the components of the room at their warehouse in Pomona, brought them down on a flatbed truck, and bolted them together at the cove.

During the 1930s, when a storm damaged the cabin, four of the couples decided to pull out of the arrangement. The two remaining families, the Parkers and the Lees, dug out the side of the bluff, moved the cabin back against it, raised and repaired the porch, and built a seawall in front. The old room became a true cottage when they added a kitchen in back and a bedroom on each side of the main room, one for each family. An indoor bathroom and one upstairs room with a small porch were added in 1940, and the cottage has remained much the same ever since. Beaches was one of very few cove cottages to stay in the same family continuously; Phyllis Parker Lowe and her daughter, Nancy, were the last tenants. The cottage currently functions as Crystal Cove's Film and Media Museum and may also be rented as a special event venue for weddings and other occasions.

TOP:
Cottage #13 is the last house at the south end of the cove.

FAR RIGHT:
Cottage #13 all dressed up for the movie *Beaches*, 1988. After production the crews removed the add-ons and returned the cottage to its original form.

RIGHT:
An untitled Roger Kuntz painting from the early 1960s (oil on canvas, 36 x 40).

65

Cottage #7

The Carter Cottage

After the schooner the Esther Buhne wrecked on Balboa Point in 1927, several new cottages sprang up at the cove, with teak wood from the shipwreck used as their main material. It's likely that #7 was among them. When Bud Carter's family bought the cottage in 1939, it had a living room, one small bedroom, a bathroom, a kitchen, and an open sun porch. The first few years of visits consisted of working weekends: the Carters used garage doors from their home in San Marino to enclose the sun porch and later built a deck. In the 1940s, when the cove's managers were no longer enforcing the palm-frond rule, Bud removed the thatching and replaced it with new board-and-batten siding. His brother, Jack, later added shingles to provide insulation for winter use. "But most of the time," Bud admitted, "we worked just to keep the place from falling apart." Obviously the work paid off; the Carters' cottage had one of the most appealing interiors at the cove. Once the final cottages on the north end of the beach have been restored, #7 will be available as an overnight rental.

LEFT:
Cottage #7 in 1928.

TOP RIGHT:
Before the palm-frond edict ended, 1940.

CENTER RIGHT:
In 1965, after the addition of a deck and shingles.

BOTTOM RIGHT:
The front room in 2001.

Cottage #7

Chapter 3

Every Night Was Saturday Night

1941 to 1962

It started every Memorial Day weekend: families from all over Southern California loaded trailers and trucks with wooden frames, large sheets of canvas, butane stoves, refrigerators, cots, portable beds, and lots of other items needed to live away from home for three months. It was difficult to explain to the neighbors where we were going and how we were going to live all summer at the beach. Driving down the highway we looked like something out of *The Grapes of Wrath.*

— Mike Fenderson —

PREVIOUS SPREAD:
A color postcard of Crystal Cove's
summer tenting from the 1940s.

ABOVE:
A roadside sign advertises the cove to
motorists, 1946. Left to right: Phyllis
Parker, Patty Gilmore, Velma Brown,
Virginia Nelson, and Nancy Edinger.

RIGHT:
Cottages and tents seen from
the cove's southern bluff.

Crystal Cove

had always been an escape from the concerns of modern life, but when World War II began, modern life intruded. The threat of attack by Japanese submarines suddenly made California's coast a dangerous place to be. Soon after the bombing of Pearl Harbor, the Japanese sharecroppers across the highway were sent to internment camps, and the roadside vegetable stands that had been a traditional stop for many cove visitors disappeared. The Japanese schoolhouse became the property of the Coast Guard, which patrolled the beach at night with dogs and used Crystal Cove for drills. "The army started training men at the far end of the beach and we watched them rappelling off the cliffs," Sheila Green, a frequent visitor to Cottage #8, later recalled. "One morning we were awakened by the noise of huge military planes conducting a practice search-and-rescue operation."

Tent camping and bonfires were declared unsafe and halted for a few years; cottagers had to abide by an 8 P.M. curfew and install regulation blackout curtains. But even in dark and dangerous times the spirit of the cove shone through. During a storm, Biddy Payne invited some of the Coast Guard boys in for tea, prompting a lecture from a commanding officer. And when Bud Carter joined the Army Air Forces, he sometimes called his parents to announce that he was about to do a flyby over the cove; they'd run outside and spell "Hi Bud" on the sand with towels.

The general store and soda fountain, which sat right on the beach, was the center of social life in the summer—not just a place to buy groceries and order lunch, but also the drop-off where cottagers received their mail. In the early evenings a windup Victrola transformed the store's wooden deck into a dance hall for cove youngsters. Some of the teenage girls followed the servicemen on their patrols at night and invited them to play volleyball during the day. "It was one of these servicemen that I met at Crystal Cove who later became my husband," said Virginia Sheeder–Mergell, whose family lived in Cottage #2.

In the late 1940s another small business opened on the bluff overlooking the cove: a roadside stand selling dried fruit, nuts, juice, and shakes. Though removed from the cottages by its location, the "shake shack," as it came to be known, became a popular hike destination for coveites and provided coveted summer jobs for cottage teens. It also gave motorists a chance to stop and observe the good life being lived on the beach below.

Tent camping returned after the war, and everything about it was bigger and better. Some people acquired army surplus tents, and others had theirs custom made. All reflected the expansive spirit of the postwar boom. Since cove families spent every weekend at the beach from Memorial Day to Labor Day—and some of the wives and children even stayed there during the workweek—the tents needed all the amenities of twentieth-century living. Some campers refused to call them tents, preferring *cabañas,* a term whose sophistication more closely mirrored that of their architecture.

Putting up such elaborate structures was an all-day activity. Campers rented trailers to haul in their supplies and invited friends and family to help with the "barn" raising. It took several people to construct a foundation—a twelve-by-twenty-four-foot box made of boards and shoveled full of sand. A subfloor of boards or Masonite followed and was finished with carpet, straw mat, or linoleum. Next the walls went up: vertical boards and crosspieces to make a frame, and over that the canvas tent.

To accommodate these architectural wonders, the cove managers during this era—the Darlingtons, Masons, and McMenomys—used a tractor to draw sand up from the shoreline and create a broad, level shelf of beach. Shower facilities and rest rooms were centralized as at any campground, but the tenters had everything else they needed inside their summer homes. Each site was wired for electricity, so most tents had a refrigerator, a hot plate, a coffee pot, and electric lights hanging from the ceiling. Some women even brought sewing machines. Butane stoves were also popular, and,

for those who had an icebox instead of a refrigerator, an iceman came down the beach every other day, selling blocks for twenty-five cents. The campers furnished their cabañas with beds, dressers, tables, and benches—then decorated with seashells, fishing nets, and palm fronds. Wires strung across the ceiling gave the space structure: hang up some drapes on shower-curtain rings, and you had private "rooms" for dressing and sleeping.

"The tenters came from all walks of life," said Mike Fenderson, a cabaña child who was the Crystal Cove lifeguard as a teen. "They were CEOs of large companies, airplane mechanics, firemen, policemen, newspaper photographers. They had very little in common until they arrived and established their community." But the group was tight since the same families returned every summer. Once you secured a spot, it was yours until you passed it on to friends or relatives.

With the arrival of summer came the seasonal opening of the store, which catered primarily to the cabaña dwellers. "The campers could in some cases buy and sell the cove," recalled Lee Van Pelt of Cottage #3, whose family ran the small business. "The people with cabins and cottages were usually in a lower income bracket." Weekday sales paid for stocking the store for the weekend, when all the profits came in. "It was really amazing how much beer could be gone through in a weekend," he said.

LEFT, TOP AND CENTER:
Each Memorial Day, tent campers erected their cabañas for another summer at the cove. The elaborate structures remained until Labor Day.

BOTTOM LEFT:
Inside the Steen family tent, which Anna (left) decorated with fabric, shells, and nautical knickknacks.

TOP:
Sandbags protected tents from high tides and created front yards for lounging.

BOTTOM:
Party time in the tents: campers assemble for an impromptu social gathering.

RIGHT:
Volleyball play continued all day.

FAR RIGHT:
Skim boarding at low tide.

Launching a catamaran.

Most tenting clans were extended families, but the occasional less-orthodox group livened up the party. Sam Gould, his son Jim, and friends Lyle Lindahl and Earl "Pinky" Brown, for instance, were bachelors who regularly applied their talent for good times on the beaches and ski slopes of California. They were also plumbers and made themselves handy at the cove. Pinky remembered the day he outfitted their tent with kitchen cabinets and a sink. A water tank with a spigot produced running water. "We had an open house that night and one of the gals said, 'What? No hot water?'" he recalled. "I didn't like that at all." So that night Pinky hatched an idea: with the burner from a water heater set on a frame under a bucket, the bachelors could build a hot-water tap. When he set up his invention, he also raised the bar for cabaña living standards. "The guys on the beach were mad at us because all the women wanted hot and cold running water," Pinky said. "I supplied a whole lot of people with water-heater burners that year."

High tides in August threatened the tent town, so everyone built low protective walls around their cabañas out of sandbags. The walls also defined a front yard for each site and made a convenient bench for guests. Furnished with umbrellas and beach chairs, the yards were the cove equivalent of parlors, where tenters lounged, read, entertained, and kept an eye on children playing in the water. At night much of the cooking took place out on the barbecue.

For all coveites, whether tenters or cottagers, life's important events were lived outside. In front of the cabañas a volleyball net saw continuous activity from sunup to sundown. Kids explored the tide pools, hunted for shells, and hiked the cliffs looking for the old hermit rumored to live there in a cardboard hut. Several families had catamarans, and launching one through the surf was a group activity. Tenters Stella and Babe Hiatt taught the cove teens to water-ski behind their outboard motorboat. One year just about everyone in the cove took a turn riding the surf in Lee Van Pelt's legendary army-surplus rubber boat. Some coveites say twelve people at a time rode it—others claim it could hold as many as thirty.

Individual sporting equipment was minimal. The only surfers were off-duty lifeguards, and their boards were simple planks of balsa wood. Bodysurfing and skin diving were more popular. There was no such thing as a wetsuit or scuba tank at the cove; fins and face masks were the only gear required. Often the diving was a preparation for dinner. Abalone were plentiful, and several of the men were excellent divers. "You would just say, 'Let's have abalone tonight,' and they'd go out and get one like going to the store for a

Every Night Was Saturday Night   1941 to 1962

Riding the waves on surf mats.

Crystal Cove Cottages

On Saturdays at four o'clock Doc Shearer (striped shirt) would announce cocktail hour with a bugle call and salute to the beloved "martini flag."

pound of hot dogs," remembered tenter Betty Steen. The wives of surf fishermen—who caught perch, corbina, and shovel-nose shark—and spearfishers, who could find halibut on command, would often make similar requests of their husbands when planning dinner. Some nights were good for hunting grunion, a small silver fish that swims up on the beach at night to spawn. Parents would let their children stay up late, and everyone would hunt the fish in the dark with flashlights, scooping them out of the shallow surf by the handful or bucketful.

Every Saturday at four o'clock—the official start of cocktail hour—tenter Doc Shearer gathered a group of campers around the flagpole outside his cabaña. Everyone saluted as Doc blew taps on his bugle and raised the flag his wife, Babe, had sewn; the black background bore the sharp white outline of a martini glass. Back home Doc led the Shriners' Top Hat Band, and sometimes the members would pay a visit and entertain the cove gang. At the very least a ukulele accompanied the nightly bonfires and sing-alongs. As Stella Hiatt put it, "Every night was Saturday night, and Saturday night was New Year's Eve."

Most inspired of all, however, were luau nights. The 1950s craze for Polynesian culture made a significant impression on coveites, who felt they lived much like carefree Pacific Islanders. Luau parties went over big. The women wore

Crystal Cove Cottages

Game wardens check to see that
Bob Davick's abalone catch is legal size. The inner tube
had a gunnysack tied to it for
storing abalone while a diver looked for more.

Game wardens counting abalone. Bob Davick and Ken Steen's huge hauls could meet legal limits if they attributed a few abalone to each of the kids who tagged along with them.

muumuus, plastic leis, and hibiscus flowers in their hair. Men garbed themselves in Hawaiian-print shirts and even sarongs. Pinky Brown preferred "formal" dress: he wore a necktie over his bare chest, with swim trunks. With all the barbecues corralled together, the tenters might have enough steaks grilling for the whole cove. After dinner they gathered around a giant fire pit dug that afternoon and drank and sang late into the night. In the morning, parents directed their children to Kate Ficken, a widowed tenter who entertained the young set with the Juice Club, offering juice, crackers, games, and books while the adults slept late.

Communal parenting embodied the cove ethos. If you were lucky enough to have landed a cottage or a tent site, you were family: good for a favor, covered in a crisis. Together the tribe worked miracles—and dispensed with emergencies in time for dinner. "Even high tides were a fun event that drew everyone out to shovel and dig trenches in front of the tents," camper Barbara Vandenberg Boatman recalled. If a tent did flood, "'Oh well,' was the attitude—no one got too terribly excited about anything getting ruined."

The outlook was similar up in the cottages, where the architectural character was settling into a casual state of repose. No new cottages were allowed after the Irvine notice of 1939, and without any stake in ownership, those living in them were not inspired to make major improvements. While communities like Emerald Bay had become posh, the buildings of Crystal Cove remained funky beach dwellings with barely more comfort and privacy than the tents. "The thin board partitions permitted no secrets at all," Sheila Green recalled of Cottage #8. "There was even a hole in the wall that separated the bathroom and kitchen, so that the person on the toilet could watch the meal preparation."

TOP LEFT:
Lifeguard Mike Fenderson and his assistant, niece Sue Cross, look out for troubled swimmers.

ABOVE:
Cooking seafood stew on the beach, c. 1960s.

RIGHT:
A festive dinner in the Steen tent: (left to right) Betty, Jan, Ken, Anna, Eric, and Margaret.

FAR RIGHT:
Umbrellas tipped on their sides create a wind block for group barbecuing.

Every Night Was Saturday Night   1941 to 1962

Crystal Cove Cottages

ABOVE:
Bob Davick and Peggy Webb,
sweethearts who met at the cove as teenagers.

LEFT:
Tenters dancing late into the night.

There was also little turnover in tenancy. As the original cottagers got older and retired, some moved to the beach full time. Others handed their cottages down to their grown children, who began to measure their summer friendships by decades and generations.

But even the cove was not immune to growth and development. California's population was soaring, and Orange County was becoming crowded. Suburban developments were filling in some of the wide-open spaces between small towns, and brand-new Disneyland, opened in 1955, was turning the orange and walnut groves of nearby Anaheim into prime tourism real estate. In 1962, responding to complaints of overcrowding on its shores, the Orange County Board of Supervisors outlawed tenting on local beaches. Without a romantic naturalist like JI, who had died in 1947, at its helm, the Irvine Company did not care to challenge the edict. The camping concession at the cove closed, and along with it the store.

The tenters, of course, were devastated. No more bonfires, no more luaus, no more summers on the sand. "When we had to leave it seemed like the end of a chapter in my life," Stella Hiatt said. "It was ten years before, emotionally, I could come back."

Donna Fenderson Sydow, Bob Oliver, and Barbara Vandenberg do the hula at a 1956 luau.

Cottage #34

The Japanese Schoolhouse

The Japanese sharecroppers who farmed on Irvine property directly inland from Crystal Cove in the 1920s and 1930s built a schoolhouse for their children in 1934. While the kids attended public school during the week, they spent Saturdays here, studying Japanese and learning the cultural traditions of their parents' native country. The building also hosted community parties, costumed kendo demonstrations, and Buddhist services. But those activities ended abruptly after the attack at Pearl Harbor, when Japanese Americans were sent to internment camps and the Coast Guard took over the building. After the war the Japanese farmers did not return, and the schoolhouse stood empty. In 1947 Ray Kuechel—with help from his politically connected nephew Thomas Kuechel, later a U.S. senator—got permission to move the house south to its current spot at Crystal Cove. Under a lease from the Irvines, the Kuechels converted it into a vacation house and later passed the lease on to Ruth Weber. The most recent tenants were Don and Marilyn Davis. Today the old schoolhouse is again a learning environment, serving as the park's Cultural Center, a meeting space for programs and events. The Cultural Center and its panoramic deck may also be rented for events.

View of the cove from the south. The schoolhouse, in its original position, is visible in the upper left corner.

The porch of Cottage #34, framed by an ivy arch.

John Cosby's *Coastal Morning* (oil on linen, 12 x 24, 2000) shows Cottage #34's position as the last cottage on the north end of the bluff.

Cottage #46

The Green Store

Right down on the sand, at the end of the Crystal Cove entrance road, sits the cove's newest cottage, built as a store in 1950. It replaced the previous store, now known as Cottage #45, which had been hauled by tractor to the entrance road and converted to a cottage after a storm damaged it. An even earlier structure, a palm-thatched snack stand, had occupied the same spot in the cove's formative days.

By the 1950s the store was a modern soda fountain with a counter and stools. It was run by Merle and Pearl Van Pelt and their son, Lee, of Cottage #3, and operated from May to September selling short-order-grill items, ice cream, penny candy, firecrackers, punch cards (lottery tickets), groceries, and supplies, primarily to tenters. With the end of tent camping in 1962, there was not enough demand to keep the store running. For a few years it was used as a cottage and then briefly became a surfboard-building shop for Rusty Makely, son of manager Russ Makely. But mostly it was used for storage, a sad state of affairs for such prime real estate.

When artist Vivian Falzetti and her husband, Doug, moved to Cottage #15 in the mid-1970s, she found she needed a studio space and arranged to lease the old store. Because of its central location the studio was hardly a tranquil retreat, but Vivian learned to simultaneously work and talk to her drop-in visitors, including the cove kids, whom she set up with art supplies, instituting informal art classes.

Once the residents moved out, the Green Store became the temporary visitors' center for the Crystal Cove Historic District. Now it provides an exhibition space for rotating exhibits on the art, culture, and natural environment of the cove.

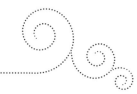

TOP RIGHT:
Lee, Merle, and Pearl Van Pelt running the soda fountain in the 1950s.

CENTER RIGHT:
The store as art studio, 2001.

BOTTOM RIGHT:
Vivian Falzetti with her grandsons, Bryan and Joseph, in the studio, 2001.

Chapter 4

An Island in Time

1963 to 1979

> Crystal Cove … is the last survivor of its type and period along the Southern California coast. Other beach colonies have become major centers of population and have lost the early character they once possessed. Only Crystal Cove remains intact and strongly conveys the sense of time and place which has disappeared from the rest of the southern coast.
>
> — National Register of Historic Places nomination form, 1978 —

Not all the cottage dwellers were sad to see the camping concession go. Some missed watching the three-ring circus provided by the tenters' activities, but others were perfectly happy to have their views unobstructed and their beach uncluttered in both summer and winter. The community was smaller now and didn't fluctuate so much with the seasons, though some residents did rent their cottages out in the summer. Meanwhile, the longevity of certain families became more established as third and fourth generations of coveites grew up on the beach.

But the end of camping signified a larger change in the region's landscape: as population density increased, Crystal Cove was becoming an anomaly. Once there had been similar beach colonies all up and down the California coast. Now these were being replaced by more up-to-date developments as owners improved their properties or sold them to developers. But since the Irvine Company owned the cottages, the cove remained as it was, while all around it orchards and fields slowly gave way to housing, commercial strips, and business parks. After JI died, his son Myford began to move the Irvine Company away from ranching and farming and toward development, building and leasing parts of the ranch as upscale suburban tracts. When Myford died in 1959, the new directors took the Irvine Company even further in that direction, creating an extensive master plan including a new city, called Irvine. JI's granddaughter Joan, who was on the board of directors, pushed the company to donate one thousand acres to the University of California for a new campus there. Embodying both traditional Irvine values and modern financial savvy, it was both a philanthropic gesture and a way to increase the value of the remaining property.

Cove residents followed such developments with a wary eye. Their always-tenuous claim became even less solid as the value of the land under them grew. Many decided it was best to keep a low profile, which wasn't too hard. The roadside signs for the camping concession had come down, highway improvements had raised the Pacific Coast Highway farther away from the cottages, and the trees around them had grown up. It was now possible to drive right past the cove and not even suspect it was there.

As long as they didn't contradict the Irvines, ask for too much, or attract too much attention, users of the cove were allowed to do pretty much what they wanted. Nude sunbathing (usually by daytrippers) was tolerated north and south of the cottages. There were still bonfires on the beach almost every night in summer, and regular visits from horseback riders passing through on their way to and from the Irvine Equestrian Center, about a mile upcoast of the cottages (some of which now had hitching posts out front). On the Fourth of July, illegal Mexican fireworks enlivened the huge celebrations, as did the glowing flotillas that coveite Bob Davick built out of wooden planks and highway flares. So many friends and relatives showed up that the private cove felt like a public beach.

With the 1960s and 1970s came an environment of casualness and the freedom to do your own thing. The arts and crafts movement, which was shaking up the staid art community in nearby Laguna, was a natural fit with the cove, where the houses themselves, with their multiple additions and building materials, were starting to look like folk-art projects. One of the biggest proponents of cove funkiness was Stan Benson, who threw beach parties that were more like crafts fairs. Anyone who showed up was invited to join in tie-dyeing, kite building, and sand-candle making on the beach. One of

PREVIOUS SPREAD:
Cove kids lighting sparklers as the sun goes down, 1975.

TOP RIGHT:
Riders from the nearby Irvine Equestrian Center were frequent visitors to the cove in the 1970s.

CENTER RIGHT:
A surprise visit from a hang-glider typifies 1970s beach antics.

BOTTOM RIGHT:
Making sand candles at one of Stan Benson's parties, 1971.

No. 009

PREVIOUS SPREAD:
Beach party preparations, 1971.

ABOVE:
A yacht club membership card. Everyone was a commodore, and the only entry requirement was that founder Jim Thobe had to like you.

ABOVE RIGHT:
The Crystal Cove Yacht Club, built from driftwood and furnished with finds from the dump, 1975.

FAR RIGHT, TOP:
On the Porch by Roger Kuntz (oil on canvas, 24 x 30, c. 1960).

FAR RIGHT, BOTTOM:
Roger Kuntz in his outdoor studio.

Stan's hand-drawn invites requested that guests contribute a dollar for kite materials and offered "special rates to senior citizens, veterans of foreign wars, retired hookers, and men paying alimony to more than one ex-wife."

Professional artists were also finding inspiration at the cove. Now it wasn't just the pristine landscape but the collection of offbeat cottages that drew them. The most famous of the regular visitors was the painter Roger Kuntz, who spent several weeks there each summer. Roger also taught painting at the Laguna Beach School of Art and Design and would often bring his classes to Crystal Cove to paint. His views of the cove—both beach scenes and interiors—capture the relaxed and genial atmosphere of this era.

It was around 1964 that another artist, this one self-styled, appeared at the cove. Allan Wallace may have started out as a handyman to manager Laura McMenomy, but his real talent quickly emerged: he could be a stealthy and somewhat malicious security guard. He stayed on in this capacity long after Laura left and became a curious fixture of cove life. Coveites weren't exactly sure where he slept, but for more than thirty-five years Allan spent most of his time outside the row of garages near the gated entrance. Uninvited guests approaching the gate—and often invited ones as well—were subject to harassment. He changed the "no trespassing" sign to read "you ARE trespassing" and posted others that offered "free towing." Whatever aggravation he caused them, residents tolerated Allan and his outbursts as another eccentricity of the cove. Those who got to know him discovered that he built sculptural furniture out of driftwood and sold pieces at Laguna's Sawdust Art Festival; a door he made even appeared on the cover of *Sunset* magazine.

But the cove's most splendid "art" installation was a conceptual work to rival one of Andy Warhol's happenings. In the early 1970s Jim Thobe, a relentless prankster, got the idea to build a yacht club on the sand in front of the cottages. "I saw all this damned wood washing up," he explained. "Driftwood, hatch covers—it was all over the place. So I said, 'What the hell? Let's make a yacht club.' I had a Hobie 16 catamaran—figured we had to have a yacht club for the boat." A thatched canopy of driftwood on the sand with a hand-painted "rest rooms" sign that pointed visitors to the ocean, the Crystal Cove Yacht Club became an instant icon, a place to gather for sunset cocktails or afternoon beers—or, on a good day, both. Artist Vivian Falzetti, of Cottage #15, designed a club T-shirt, and Thobe came up with his most brilliant idea yet: printed membership cards bearing an official-looking logo. Since yachting organizations

Crystal Cove Cottages

PREVIOUS SPREAD:
A handmade boardwalk leads to
cottages at the north end of the cove,
where the road does not reach.

ABOVE:
Roger Kuntz's *Tide Pools*
(oil on canvas, 40 x 48, 1957) shows his wife,
Margaret, and daughter, Mary, at Crystal Cove.

RIGHT:
Unofficial security guard
Allan Wallace outside the garages, 1976.

around the world have a policy of reciprocation, Thobe and other members successfully used their counterfeit cards to enter private clubs from Hawaii to New Zealand.

Most of the cove's popular recreational activities continued, although diving and fishing were curtailed by reduced sea life populations. Surfing joined the list of pastimes, even though the cove's waves were not the best for the sport (not that this stopped teens like Dale Carter, Rusty Makely, and Jeff Killen, who were often up by dawn to ply their local waves before heading to better breaks). The surf at the cove was actually much better suited to bodysurfing. "There is something about the shore break at Crystal Cove that makes it the easiest place I know to bodysurf," coveite Shari Pilaria said. "There were many summer days that ended too soon, as my extended family would all be out bodysurfing until dark." But the cove's chief sport continued to be volleyball, presided over by Jack Shirley, also known as the "Mayor of Crystal Cove." "We lived and—almost literally—died for volleyball," said Jack's stepson, Mahlon Vail. "We played for hours and hours, only breaking to eat, swim, and get more beer. The only rule was that you could not tear down the net."

The cove kids rode skim boards, built sand castles, and explored the tide pools, priding themselves on feet callused from scrambling over barnacle-crusted rocks. Craig Benson remembered the summer morning in the early 1960s when a gang of kids discovered a pelican whose throat had been punctured by fish hooks. The kids nursed the wounded bird back to health with the help of the cove's resident veterinarian, Francis "Shorty" Turner, "a short, lean, extremely weathered man who had lost his right thumb to an alligator that he'd once kept as a pet," Craig recalled. Shorty and his wife, Sandy, kept a menagerie of wounded or stray animals in their cottage, including Mr. Flip, a rescued sea lion that followed Shorty everywhere. The two animal lovers also took it upon themselves to feed the cove's feral cat community.

The cove volleyball net was a work of art, meticulously repaired with scraps of rope that washed up on the beach.

"In those days, only a handful of people were year-rounders like us Bensons," Craig recalled. "Most were widows who lost their husbands in the Great War or simply outlived them. They all had old-timey names such as Lillian Arnold, Rose Bartel, May Banneman, Biddy Payne, and Pearl Van Pelt." There was a cadre of winter weekenders as well—indeed for some coveites, the off-season was the preferred time of year. Christine Shirley, a Los Angeles teacher who herded her family down to the cove *every* weekend, rain or shine, wrote that she most relished stormy nights—"the fire crackling in the fireplace, the shuffle of the cards, the clink of ice in the glasses, and the raindrops on the tar paper roof."

"The wintertime denizens of the cove were all of our closest friends," said Mahlon Vail, Christine's son. "We considered ourselves hearty, stalwart souls, beachcombers, enjoyers of solitude who, however, sought each other's company to share a fire, a story, and a warming libation. It was so very enjoyable on those pitch-black winter evenings to feel your way down to the sand and head up the beach searching for lighted cottages."

Coveites also sought each other out in times of crisis. A storm in February 1969 washed out the walkway to Cottage #40 and left an eight-foot drop at the front door. "We were on the edge of panic when Stan Benson, who owned a tire company, brought a truckload of junk tires," Jeanette Dillinger reported in 1978. "We rolled them down the bank, passed them hand to hand, and stacked them down in the bottom of the washout. Since then, al-

The cottages in 1977: still secluded.

though we have lost moderate amounts of the front and side yard, the tires continue to protect from serious damage."

The destruction from another heavy rain, in 1967, was sadly irreparable, and it highlighted for the coveites just who was in charge, in case they had forgotten. "There had been a long, slow rain lasting many days," recalled Betty Ford McGraw of Cottage #25. "When we came down to the cottage from Pasadena, the hill behind the house had moved toward the sea. Our toilet was tipped to the side and the cement in the shower was cracked. At Charlotte Kortlander's house, next door to the north, the electric wires had snapped and the cement behind the house was buckled and tilted." The Irvine Company put signs on these two cottages saying that they were not to be used. The McGraws complied, and their cottage was later repaired. But Charlotte made the mistake of writing a complaint to the Irvine Company on stationery from the legal office where she worked. "In three days," Betty recalled, "her house was demolished and removed except for the wooden 'Kortlander' sign."

Coveites were outraged by this act but not exactly surprised. They had all become familiar with Irvine policy—and power—the minute they signed their leases. "I remember Mom driving out to the Irvine office to sign the paperwork," Mahlon recalled. "The Irvine Company lady looked sternly at us and asked if we realized that we were buying nothing, that our tenancy was at their convenience, and that we had no property rights. Mom said, 'Where do I sign and where's the gate key?'"

As houses changed hands, coveites tried to keep them in the family. Christine knew Crystal Cove from spending summers with her cousins the Van Wycks, in Cottage #12. The Rowlands in Cottage #27 were cousins of the Pilarias in #17. Laura McMenomy passed her management position on to her nephew, Russ Makely, and rented to her niece, Nancy Killen. Though most new residents paid the previous "owner" a substantial amount of money, it was not a sale price but essentially a finder's fee. This added to a sense of ownership, however, especially among younger generations of coveites who had distinct memories of their parents paying for the family cottage, and in many cases how much they had paid. For some it was hard to understand later that their families had never actually owned the cottages—at least not since the Irvines had forced the quitclaim back in 1940.

"The surprising thing is that we have a very real community of people; there are four and five generations of some families in the cove," Christine wrote in the 1970s, when she began to document the history of Crystal Cove. "I have to question how such a long-standing community could exist in a place where there are only temporary leases. How is it that we get along so well when we have no property interest in the place? One thinks of Karl Marx!"

This was in extreme and even ironic contrast to the "planned communities" that the Irvine Company was starting to develop nearby, particularly the new city of Irvine, eight miles inland from Crystal Cove. Engineered by an elaborate

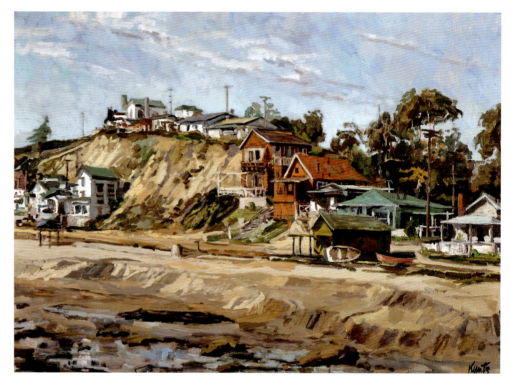

View from Sea by Roger Kuntz (oil on canvas, 30 x 40, 1973).

Interior of Artist's Home by
Roger Kuntz (oil on canvas, 40 x 50, c. 1970).

Coffee-can garden outside cottage 23.

master plan, Irvine was the antithesis of the cove community: clean, modern, uniform, and premeditated to the last detail. Mid-century highway-building programs were adding more ways to get around Orange County—I-5, I-405, and smaller freeways named after the cities of Garden Grove, Costa Mesa, Orange, and Riverside. As Christine wrote at the time, "One feels cultural shock when returning from the highly developed areas of Orange County to the cove—an 'un-planned Irvine community,' as we've so often called it."

While it was charting out a long-term future vision for its new communities, the Irvine Company meanwhile would not allow improvements at the cove. Residents did undertake surreptitious construction projects, but accommodations generally remained primitive: the septic tanks were always backing up, skunks and raccoons got into the garbage cans, and the water pressure was so low that the McMenomys had to turn their garden hose off any time their neighbor wanted to take a shower. In Cottage #21 the electric current was only 15 amps; if the toaster and iron were on at the same time, the fuse would blow. Doug Falzetti commemorated the cove's quirks with a sign he hung on the old store, which had become his wife Vivian's art studio: "Crystal Cove standard time. Please turn your clocks back to 1930."

Residents knew that the future of their tenancy was even shakier than the cottages themselves. If the Irvine Company didn't want to make improvements, it probably had something else in mind for the property. Sure enough, word leaked out about plans for a European-style resort project. But Irvine was not in a position to do something so bold. Voter approval of the 1972 California Coastal Act clearly signaled that Californians wanted their beaches preserved, not developed. Add to that several battles with environmental groups over other Irvine developments, and the company suddenly found it needed to burnish its public image. As a result, parkland became a significant component of the revised 1973 master plan for the ranch. That year the Irvine Company attempted to sell to the California Department of Parks and Recreation nearly two thousand acres of coastal property from Corona del Mar to Laguna, including Crystal Cove. But shareholders Joan Irvine Smith and her mother, Athalie Clarke, held up the deal with a lawsuit claiming that the price offered by the state—$7.5 million—was far below value. Critics said the women were just trying to increase the value of their stock, but Joan asserted that she was protecting her family's legacy. Similar sweet deals for government agencies had turned into boondoggles; a small parcel of Irvine property previously sold to the state parks department had become a gated community, and one sold to Newport Beach in 1946 to become a city park was now a private club. A fairer price, she argued, would lower the chances of backroom bargains.

An Island in Time 1963 to 1979

Thirty-Three by Roger Kuntz
(oil on canvas, 36 x 40, 1957).

Though frustrated by their inability to make improvements, a handful of coveites came to recognize the Irvine Company's restrictions as a potential buttress to their uncertain status. Neglect of the cottages had become an unintentional act of historic preservation at a time when the landmarks movement was gaining momentum. The National Register of Historic Places, initiated by the federal government in 1966, was starting to gain cachet as a community tool.

Coveite Martha Padve remembered the moment when a Crystal Cove preservation movement sprang into being. "It was early October 1976, one of those sparkly Sundays we often have at Crystal Cove in the fall of the year," she said. "I was sitting on the deck of our cottage with Russ Makely, discussing the eternally fascinating and frightening subject of our future. People from the California Department of Parks and Recreation had been poking around again that summer. 'You know what I think?' Russ said. 'I think we might have a chance of keeping this place if it was made a landmark.'" Martha, who had been involved in the formation of the Pasadena Cultural Heritage Commission, had been having the same thought.

Martha gathered a group of residents and some experts: Deborah

An Island in Time   1963 to 1979

FAR LEFT:
After camping ended, coveites began to cherish their privacy.

ABOVE LEFT:
Mailbox and road signs at the entrance to the cove, 1976.

ABOVE RIGHT:
A jade plant turns red in the sun.

Feldman, who was creating Pasadena's heritage program; Pam Hallen, an Orange County cultural heritage commissioner; and Ilse Byrnes, chairman of the Historic Landmark Committee of the San Juan Capistrano Historical Society. Once they heard the cove's story—and its connections to the California impressionist art movement, early moviemaking, rumrunning, agriculture, and postwar recreation—these professionals assured Martha that she had a landmark on her hands.

Then Martha tapped Christine Shirley, who happened to be a historian with degrees from Stanford and UCLA. The two organized residents' association meetings and letter-writing campaigns, produced a newsletter, and mailed a questionnaire to all the residents, seeking historical information to bolster an application to the National Register. The last step was risky because it meant letting all of the other coveites know what they were up to; it also asked, in writing, for their involvement. "The residents were terrified of any action that brought attention to the cove," Martha explained, "fearful of incurring the wrath of the powerful Irvine Company." But the questionnaire resulted in reams of valuable cove family histories and anecdotes (some of which have been used as research material for this book). Arguing for the cove as "the last intact example of California beach vernacular architecture" amid a sea of encroaching development, the team worked feverishly to build a convincing case. "Our application was considered at the State Historic Preservation Commission in Alameda on May 10, 1978," Martha later wrote. "A representative of the Irvine Company vigorously opposed our proposal. The Commission overwhelmingly voted in favor of it."

But the victory was a Pyrrhic one. In December 1979, the Irvine Company and Joan Irvine Smith finally resolved their litigation when the company negotiated a new price with state parks: the state would buy 1,898 acres of Irvine coastal property—including Crystal Cove—for $32.6 million, the highest price ever paid for a single parkland purchase. A coastal park had been JI's vision decades before, and now it would finally happen; there would be no high-end tract homes here, no luxury resort. But the fate of the coveites was unclear. The parks department claimed it didn't want to cause them hardship, but it also admitted that there was extreme pressure from state legislators to convert the cottages into overnight rentals for the public. The sale had protected the cottages from being overrun by commercial development, but in time it would come to mean the end of the community itself.

RIGHT:
Patio furniture overgrown with ice plant becomes art with the addition of a Beethoven bust.

BELOW:
Signage on the front of Cottage #24.

An Island in Time   1963 to 1979

Cottage #14

The McCloskey Cottage

Cottage #14 was built in 1931 by Edith Henning, secretary to the legendary movie makeup artist Max Factor. Edith fell in love with the cove during a film shoot and decided to retire there. She first tented on the site, and then built a palm-frond hut on a slab of concrete. Additions in the 1930s and 1940s created upstairs bedrooms, the garage, and the deck.

Jane and Wally McCloskey bought the cottage in 1961 and made major changes. A carpenter suggested that they push it on down the hill and start over, but Wally, a contractor, braced, rewired, and replumbed the cottage to a construction standard far surpassing that of most other cove cottages. When the McCloskeys' granddaughter Jane and her family moved to the house full time, she continued to upgrade and add personal touches, including wall stencils in the kitchen. This cottage now serves as an overnight rental and is affectionately referred to as the South Beach Suite.

NEAR RIGHT:
Number 14 (oil on canvas, 36 x 24, 1978) by Bonnie Gregory.

TOP RIGHT:
Edith Henning and friends in front of Cottage #14, 1930s.

BOTTOM RIGHT:
Hand-painted stenciling and an old-fashioned stove inside Cottage #14.

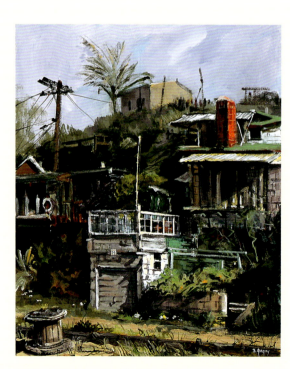

Cottage #14

Cottage #27

The Rowland Cottage

Perched on the bluff, above a winding set of brick stairs, dark-shingled #27 has more landscaping than most of the cottages and is a favorite of *plein air* painters. The steep pitched roof is unusual for the cove and allows for a high-ceilinged main room and a sleeping loft. The cottage was built in 1931 by Elsie Bantley, Margaret Orndorf, Ruth Hepner, and Dorothy Sproul, coworkers at Azusa Valley Savings Bank who had previously owned Cottage #2. They named their new digs "Elmarudor," using the first few letters from each of their first names. The cottage's most recent residents, Cinco and Edie Rowland, say it was almost unchanged from 1931 until they took over the lease in 1978. The Rowlands made only one significant change. In 1980, when a wrecked cabin cruiser washed ashore, Cinco liberated its mahogany cabinetry and completely reoutfitted their kitchen. Today Cottage #27 is one of the cottages used for overnight rentals and has been christened the Dive Shack after Cinco's long-standing tradition of spearfishing for halibut.

Gelatin molds as interior design.

Cinco and Edie Rowland in their nautical-themed living room, 2001.

Cottage #27

Three of Cottage #27's first owners, 1931.

Shingles have replaced palm fronds, but little else has changed.

Chapter 5

A Modern-Day Village

1980 to 2001

Before my mother died we would often drive over the Newport Coast Road and look down on the coast, and she would say to me, "Now dear, you know your grandfather wanted this to be a park, your father wanted it to be a park, and I want it to be a park. You must see that it remains a park for the people forever."

— Joan Irvine Smith —

The new park was called

Crystal Cove State Park, although it took in quite a bit more than the twelve-acre neighborhood of cottages. The name Crystal Cove now referred to a 1,898-acre area encompassing 3.2 miles of beach sheltered by bluffs, terraces of coastal sage scrub habitat, and the inland wilderness of El Moro Canyon. By 1981 two more acquisitions brought the acreage to twenty-eight hundred.

Though the cove may have looked much the same, life was different after the parks department took over. The relaxed atmosphere gave way to regulations: no bonfires, no horses, no dogs off leash. The yacht club, which had washed out and been rebuilt many times, was declared unsafe and taken down. A newly paved parking lot across the highway welcomed day visitors where Allan's signs had previously scared them off. There were suddenly more people on the beach—and gradually fewer animals and shells in the tide pools.

The collection of cottages was now referred to as the Crystal Cove State Park Historic District, and there was heated discussion about what should be done with them and the people who had lived in them for so long. Locals who had eyed the cove enviously for years started clamoring for the eviction of the residents. State officials agreed, saying that the public had paid a lot for this park and should have full benefit of its use. The coveites received their first eviction notices in 1979. The residents' association hired lawyers and waged a protracted legal battle that,

PREVIOUS SPREAD:
A collection of surfboards behind the office.

LEFT:
Sea lions frolicking in the cove's kelp beds.

Abalone Point by John Cosby (oil on linen, 18 x 24, 2001) shows the southern stretch of Crystal Cove State Park.

Crystal Cove Cottages

Bottlenose dolphins are regular
visitors to the cove's pristine waters.

in 1983, resulted in a ten-year lease extension. In exchange they gave up their rights to any relocation benefits, believing that it was more important to stay at the cove as long as possible.

Despite these downsides, a dedicated park was an important anchor for the stretch of land from Corona del Mar to Laguna, now the last undeveloped piece of coastline in Orange County. The Irvine Company still owned nine thousand acres of this strip and in the 1980s developed an extensive plan for hotels, retail stores, and luxury homes—twenty-six hundred of them—just outside the park's borders. By the mid-1990s the cove had its first immediate neighbors, two eighteen-hole golf courses, later joined by Marriott timeshare condos and a large retail center of high-end stores and restaurants named, to the great irritation of coveites, the Crystal Cove Promenade.

Fortunately the growing environmental movement was simultaneously bringing more protection to the cove's natural resources. The offshore area along the park was already protected by the state water board as an "area of special biological significance," and the California Department of Fish and Game had classified it as a marine life refuge—designations that controlled what humans could dump into and take out of the water. The conventional wisdom about parks was evolving to include underwater areas as resources that should be protected, enjoyed, and better understood. Thus eleven hundred offshore acres, to the 120-foot depth line, were declared the Crystal Cove Underwater Park, one of just seventeen underwater state parks noted for significant "submerged resources" of interest to divers. In the cove's case those resources were its substantial reefs and the sea life they supported. But with increased attention focused on the waters, it came to mean historical artifacts as well. Divers

An orange spotted nudibranch.

A cryptic kelp crab.

located the 1949 crash site of a U.S. Navy F4U Corsair fighter plane off Reef Point, about a mile downcoast from the cottages, and recovered a stone pestle used by native inhabitants as a grinding tool. State park staff members also discovered a 150-year-old kedge-style iron anchor off Pelican Point and later placed two massive admiralty-style anchors from the same era in the underwater park as examples of local maritime history.

But the greatest offshore discovery was one made in the early 1980s by marine biologist Dennis Kelly, a professor at Orange Coast College who leads the Coastal Dolphin Survey Project. One day while he was observing bottlenose dolphins at the cove, Dennis noticed a pod of them floating on the surface of the water in the form of a circle, their beaks pointing inward. Another dolphin floated in the middle of the ring. "My initial hypothesis was that the dolphins were giving assistance to an ailing comrade and preventing it from drifting into shore," he said. "When, much later, the dolphin in the circle submerged with the others only to return to the surface with a tiny neonate next to it and subsequently began nursing, I realized that this was something entirely different." Dennis had discovered how dolphins give birth. Finding no similar observations in the scientific literature on the bottlenose dolphin birthing behavior, he embarked on a sixteen-year mission to gather data and publish his findings, enlisting help from coveites. "All the while, the human residents at Crystal Cove kept a watchful and protective eye on the dolphins, and reported their observations and concerns to me," Dennis said. "The residents of Crystal Cove acted like citizen rangers long before the park service hired actual rangers to patrol the beaches. It was a special and very symbiotic relationship that evolved over decades. Crystal Cove was a safe haven for both dolphins and people."

Dennis felt that the coveites were the best attendants of this fragile place, and the coveites agreed. Not only did they loathe the idea of moving out for their own sakes, but they also feared what would happen to the cottages, the tide pools, and the waters if they did. A 1982 state park general plan called for historically sensitive upgrades of the cottages for uses including overnight rentals, hostels, a visitors' center, concessions, and house museums, and it was still the state's plan

The bottlenose dolphin's birthing behavior was first observed at Crystal Cove.

A Spanish shawl nudibranch.

to complete this conversion in 1993, when the residents' lease extension expired. The state parks department argued that the land had been purchased with tax dollars for this purpose and to not convert it would be to betray the public's trust. Residents countered that the state could never afford to bring the ramshackle cottages up to code. They also believed that no one was better qualified to maintain the homes' historic qualities than those who had given them their charm in the first place. "These places were never built to any code standards," Al Willinger of Cottage #30 told the *Los Angeles Times* in 1988. "The only way they've lasted is through the constant, loving attention of the people who live here." The paper also noted that Al had had to jack up and brace his home every couple of years to keep it from falling down the hill. Coveites referred to it as the "Tiltin' Hilton."

Under state regulations, coveites were allowed to make only "of kind" repairs—ones that replaced existing materials exactly—and they had to get permits to do even that much. But the bureaucratic red tape was too much for a community built on the do-it-yourself ethos. When permits were denied, secret improvements happened anyway, often undertaken at night and camouflaged with a dull shade of paint the coveites called "disappearing brown" because it blended so well with the more historic bits and pieces. They shared tools, hardware, and advice freely, often magically finding the exact parts they needed in the old garages by the entrance gate.

The community had clearly strengthened in response to the state's presence. After so many generations together the coveites had become more a family than a community, a modern-day village—some even called it a tribe. The uniqueness of Crystal Cove, they realized, was as much about the people as the place. "When at the cove, everyone hated to leave," recalled former tent camper Stella Hiatt, who had bought Cottage #42 in the 1970s. "If someone was cooking and discovered a lacking ingredient, they would go from cottage to cottage instead of going to the grocery store. If someone else was fixing something that required a special part, they wouldn't go to a hardware store; some neighbor would come up with something that would work." When storms washed out the boardwalk or auto bridge, the state might drag its heels approving repairs. Coveites would chip in the money, fix it themselves, and have a potluck dinner afterward. Even legal issues were handled cove style; the fundraisers for the residents' many lawsuits were theme parties, with picnic tables on the beach, a bar outside Vivian Falzetti's studio, and a bandstand in the driveway of Cottage #2. "Most popular were the old-time rock 'n' roll parties," Vivian recalled, "where 'Elvis' would show up in Cinco Rowland's Cadillac convertible and entertain into the wee hours."

Thanks to the drama inherent in the fight between the residents and the state, the cove had become a regular news item in the local papers. It also received considerable attention when it was chosen as a location for the 1988 Bette Midler film *Beaches*. And art patrons were noticing that it had become hard to find a gallery or art show in Laguna without at least one painting of the cottages.

Though the cove was no longer a secret, time there continued to feel as if it were standing still. In the early 1980s the community clock caught fire and no one bothered to fix it. From then on it was permanently set at a few minutes to four, the perfect time of day: early enough to still get in a walk or a swim but late enough for cocktails, if that was your preferred form of entertainment. As Joan Baxter, of Cottage #18, put it, "We did not need a clock. We knew it was midmorning when the dolphins made their way south and late afternoon when they headed north again. When Catalina became visible as the sun disappeared behind it, it was time for the family to gather for stories and hot chocolate on the porch."

But time was ticking away for the parks department. Some of the cottages were becoming decrepit, and as long as the

ABOVE:
1980s installation art by Jim Thobe.

LEFT:
Found-object mobile made by Francine Rippy of Cottage #18.

Crystal Cove Cottages

A Modern-Day Village   1980 to 2001

ABOVE:
Christmas Eve at Crystal Cove
(watercolor, 11 x 17, 1996) by Beatrice Anderson shows
the cove's decorated tree and lighted radio tower.

LEFT:
Crystal Cove at Christmas,
with an enormous tree decorated via cherry picker.

127

coveites were in residence there was always the possibility of further legal wrangling, which made contractors reluctant to bid on the planned renovation. Eventually parks officials stopped allowing any turnover of the cottages, as older residents died, or those who disagreed with the new policies moved out. Some cottages became vacant and fell into disrepair, and a few of them were broken into and vandalized. None of this gave the remaining residents confidence that their own homes would be well looked after if they left—instead it fueled their argument that they should stay in the cottages up until the moment work on the renovation began. In late June 1993, with a few days left before their scheduled eviction, the coveites got a last-minute reprieve: Governor Pete Wilson signed a state budget that included $500,000 for a renovation study and allowed residents to stay two and a half years while that work was being done. When that extension expired, on New Year's Eve 1995, there was still no construction schedule in place, and residents simply refused to leave. Soon they filed and won another lawsuit insisting they be allowed to stay until renovation started. By the late 1990s, additional extensions had put them on month-to-month leases. They could be asked to leave at any time.

Despite the threats to its future, it seemed at times that someone was looking out for the cove. On October 27, 1993, brush fires fanned by Santa Ana winds swept through Southern California. Of the fourteen fires, the largest was in Orange County; it destroyed 366 homes and nearly seventeen thousand acres—and it came dangerously close to the cove. As the flames crested the hills across the Pacific Coast Highway, coveites cut weeds and tamped out embers with shovels, moved furniture to the sand in case the cottages burned, packed what they could in their cars, and drove away, in their hearts kissing Crystal Cove good-bye. But at about nine o'clock that night, as the last few coveites were evacuating, the wind shifted and the cove was miraculously spared.

Unsure of how much time they had left, coveites began spending every possible moment at the cove. Those who were able to do so moved in full time; others started coming down for every important occasion. Couples got married on the beach and honeymooned in the cottages. The Falzettis' grandchildren were born in Cottage #15. To make sure future generations understood their connection to the cove, children were given appropriate names: Stephen and Marie Davick's daughter is Crystal, and Craig Benson's is Marina. The end of life was mourned and celebrated here as well, and ashes were sometimes scattered off the rocks or at an off-shore buoy. Magically, a pod of dolphins was often in attendance at these events.

New holiday rituals joined the more traditional ones. Doug and Vivian Falzetti hosted a casino night every New Year's Eve to keep the young people from driving into town. And at Easter there were egg hunts on the beach—with Bloody Marys served in egg-shaped plastic panty hose containers for the adults. But the most spectacular holiday was Christmas, when Laura Davick decorated the cove with thousands of tiny white lights, a thirty-five-foot tree on the sand, and a lighted

LEFT:
Coveites prepare a shrimp boil for one of their many fund-raising events.

BELOW:
Spear fisherman Cinco Rowland "shopping" for dinner.

star at the top of the TV antenna on the bluff. Today the holiday tree lighting at Crystal Cove continues as a public event held on the first Saturday of December.

In the mid-1990s the parks department completed its study, concluding that rehabilitation of the cottages should go forward as planned but suggesting a public-private partnership for funding. In other words, the state had nowhere near the money it would take to refurbish the weathered, foundationless cottages into public facilities. A request for proposals went out in 1995. The plan chosen the following year was not made public until after the contract was signed: a $35 million "eco-resort" that would turn the cottages into historically themed luxury accommodations renting for $375 to $700 a night. There would have been valet parking, a fitness center, a restaurant, and three swimming pools. Some of the cottages would have been torn down and replaced with "cottage-like structures." Though the developer promised that the public would still be able to use the beach, paying guests would have had priority at the new facilities.

The outrage was immediate and fierce—the public had not been involved in the decision-making in any way. Environmentalists and historic preservationists questioned the high level of development—and whether it would truly uphold the preservation values it espoused. Public-access advocates pointed out that most Californians would be barred from the park by price alone and worried that it set a dangerous precedent for funding cash-strapped parks by turning them into for-profit enterprises. Coveites said it sounded like the "Disneyfication" of a place that had always been the opposite of a commercial venture. For the first time, open-space advocates and coveites agreed: whatever was going to happen to Crystal Cove, it surely shouldn't be this.

But change was starting to feel inevitable. Construction had begun on the Irvine Company's latest development of upscale homes, directly across the highway from the cove. The land that the Japanese sharecroppers had once farmed would now hold vast multimillion-dollar

RIGHT:
The community clock, permanently stopped just before four.

FAR RIGHT:
Cottage #28, one of the homes left vacant in the 1990s.

Crystal Cove Cottages

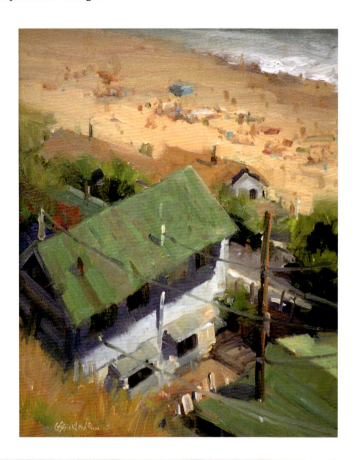
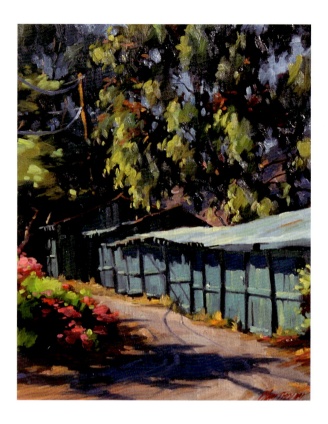

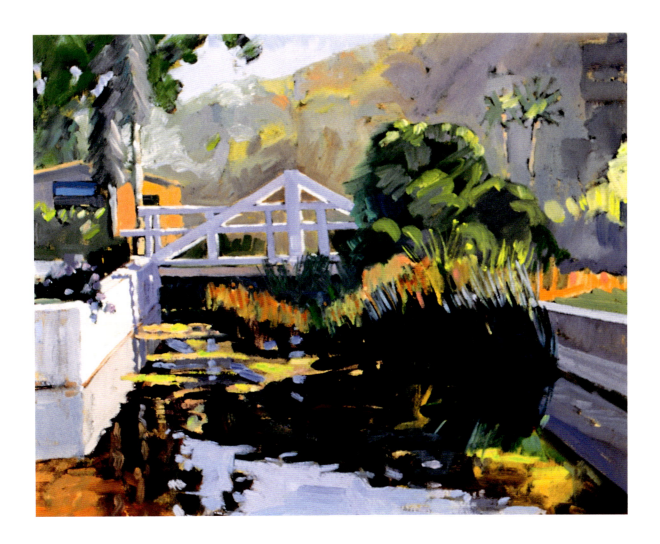

FAR LEFT, TOP:
George Strickland painted *Van Wyck House from Above* (oil on canvas, 16 x 12) on July 8, 2001, the residents' last day at the cove.

TOP LEFT:
Michael Obermeyer's *Crystal Cove Garages* (oil on canvas, 20 x 16, 2001).

LEFT:
Mariana Donahue of Cottage #1 is the subject of *Beach Shadows* (oil on canvas, 8 x 10, 2002) by Camille Przewodek.

TOP RIGHT:
An untitled painting of the auto bridge over Los Trancos Creek by Richard Rice (oil on canvas, 11 x 14, 2003).

RIGHT:
In 2001, Anita Hampton's *A Gray Day at Crystal Cove* (oil on linen, 16 x 20, 2001) won first prize at Images of Crystal Cove, a painting event to benefit the cove.

villas. As the frames went up, coveites were chagrined to note that they were visible from the beach. Crystal Cove's locked-in-time feeling was finally being chipped away.

Determined to protect what remained, Laura Davick, who grew up in Cottage #2, formed the Alliance to Rescue Crystal Cove in 1999. (Later the organization became the Crystal Cove Alliance, which put in place the infrastructure to support open access to the park, affordable overnight cottage rentals, and education and conservation programs. Known today as the Crystal Cove Conservancy, this group is now the nonprofit partner that supports Crystal Cove State Park.) The immediate concern appeared to be the resort, but in August 2000 another problem crept over the hill. Laura noticed water pooling on the beach at the end of Los Trancos Creek, though the creek had always been dry in summer. She discovered there were eight locations in Crystal Cove that had continuous runoff coming across the beach. On a hunch, she put on some old clothes, grabbed a flashlight and her camera and climbed into the box culvert that drains runoff from the inland hills. Looking around underground, she saw a network of pipes connected to the one she stood in. The box culvert, and other areas in the park, were dumping construction runoff into the cove's supposedly protected waters.

Teaming with Garry Brown, of Orange County CoastKeeper, and Susan Jordan, from the League for Coastal Protection, the Alliance reported Laura's findings to the Santa Ana Regional Water Quality Control Board and other agencies. The new construction was clearly the cause of the increased runoff, but the board's investigations revealed that other sources were tied into the pipe as well: El Morro Elementary School, Pacific Coast Highway and the cottages' ancient septic system. The board sent a cease-and-desist order to the school, the transportation department, and the parks department and gave them two years to comply. (As a result of these efforts, today all urban runoff in the area is diverted to the county sewer system.)

Faced with such environmental and political realities, Laura started to rethink what it might mean to save the cove. If the residents did indeed have to move out, what should happen to the cottages? Soon the Alliance began advocating an alternative vision to the resort: open the cottages to the public but keep the rustic feel of the cove intact—and focus on celebrating its natural and historic resources. The new plan would renovate the cottages and turn some into facilities for environmental education, marine research, or arts and cultural uses; some into dorm-style hostels; and others into overnight rentals—at a rate the average Californian could easily afford.

Criticism of the resort plan was now coming from many camps, including Laguna's considerable artist community and powerful environmental organizations such as the Sierra Club, the Natural Resources Defense Council, the Laguna Canyon Conservancy, Laguna Greenbelt, Friends of Harbors, Beaches and Parks, Friends of the Newport Coast, the League for Coastal Protection, the

An old boat adrift on a sea of greenery.

Crystal Cove Cottages

Resident surfers gather outside the store before the commemorative paddle-out on their last Fourth of July at the cove, 2001.

Coveites gather for a final family photo.

Nature Conservancy, and the Surfrider Foundation. Aware that they had a growing PR problem on their hands, parks officials decided to hold a public-information meeting to try and bolster the public image of the resort. Just weeks before the meeting, Laura got a call from someone who would turn out to be a powerful ally: Joan Irvine Smith. Having believed all along that the state would attempt to lease the park to developers, Smith was determined to do what she could to stop it.

The forces were aligning against the resort, and on January 18, 2001, they turned out en masse: six-hundred irate people attended the public meeting to wave protest signs and shout down the developer and parks officials, chanting "No resort!" Among them was Joan Irvine Smith, who, cheered on by the crowd, pronounced that the park must be for the people. Stunned by the outcry, parks officials backed down. It helped that their boss, Governor Gray Davis, had been elected after the plan was approved; the resort was now cast as a cynical idea from a previous administration. After 16 months of work to stop the resort, Laura received a call that would forever terminate the luxury resort plan. Within a month, the California Coastal Conservancy, a state agency, agreed to contribute $2 million to buy out the developer, and the resort plan was abandoned.

But the coveites' rejoicing was cut short. A flyer handed out at the meeting noted that eviction notices were already being sent to the cottage residents. The notices arrived within weeks. The parks department, citing the cease-and-desist order from the regional water board, claimed it needed the cottages empty in order to upgrade the septic-tank system. Knowing that the runoff problems had only arisen after the start of construction across the highway, residents felt it was an excuse to get them out, but there was nothing they could do. They had given up the right to file another lawsuit when they'd signed their last lease.

The coveites were crushed to realize that the end of their eighty-year idyll had finally arrived—and they were profoundly concerned that there was now no plan in place for the future of the cottages. Meanwhile, Laura's alternative plan was gaining steam, but there was no money to pay for it. Joan Irvine Smith lent her support to the effort, and together these passionate advocates for an open, accessible, and protected Crystal Cove State Park worked to move the new plan forward. Members of the Laguna Plein Air Painters Association, which has always held preservation of the natural landscape as one of its core values, offered their skills for a gallery show and painting sale to benefit the cove. The future of Crystal Cove was not certain, but it was clear that all of Orange County would be watching closely.

Prevailing on the parks department to let them have one more Fourth of July celebration at the cove, the residents consented to move out on July 8, 2001. On the Fourth the beach was packed with coveites and their friends and extended families. Old timers from the tenting days returned for a reunion, a live band entertained the crowd, and the cove's resident surfers performed a symbolic group paddle-out. By all accounts, it was Crystal Cove's biggest blowout yet.

Garages at the entrance to Crystal Cove. Any tool or material needed for a repair could be found in the garages, including the keys to a piano that Danny Falzetti found discarded in the creek bed.

The hills behind the cove.

But another gathering would prove to be the coveites' real good-bye. A few days before the move out, Stella Hiatt got an idea. Over the years she had developed a ritual with Cinda Combs, of Cottage #6: every morning at seven o'clock, in all seasons and weather, the two women swam out to the buoy anchored about a hundred feet off shore. "It wasn't just the swim itself that made the buoy our destination," Stella said. "Cinda, like me, is a widow, and the ashes of both of our husbands were scattered at sea near the buoy. On special occasions we would take a few roses with us, and have our own private ceremony, tossing the flowers and thinking our own private thoughts." Stella recognized that her grief over leaving the cove—which she had been visiting since a 1938 spring-break visit with her first boyfriend—deserved a similar ritual: why not scatter a rose for each cottage? Cinda, whose grandmother (a cousin of Jose Andres Sepulveda, the cove's first owner) had bought Cottage #6 just after World War II, agreed. They invited the other coveites to join them and bought dozens of long-stemmed roses, planning to ferry them to the buoy in an inflatable boat.

On the morning of July 8, before the moving trucks arrived, the people of Crystal Cove set down their boxes and packing tape and enjoyed one last celebration together. "When we went down to the shore to take the boat out, we were overwhelmed by the company that had joined us," Stella said. "Everyone wanted to participate in this final ceremony." Word of the plan had spread, and the crowd included not just residents but plein air painters and other fans of the cove, some bringing flowers of their own. "There were men, women, and children—some swimming, some on boogie boards, some on surfboards," Stella recalled. "When we arrived at the buoy, each person tossed a rose and offered a special prayer or farewell words to the place we all loved so dearly. Voices cracked, tears flowed, and all of the roses and other flowers floated on the ocean around us. The memory will remain with me always. It was truly a fitting and proper farewell."

Cinda Combs and Stella Hiatt taking their daily 7 A.M. swim out to the buoy.

Cottage #11

The Gabriel Cottage

Cottage #11 was built in the late 1920s by Cecil Payne—a structural engineer—for his wife, Bitty. She specifically requested that their children have separate quarters upstairs, with their own external staircase, so their comings and goings wouldn't bother her. Cecil constructed the house in increments with shipwright skill. He made additions over the years but unified the agglomeration of extensions, with their many types of roofs, by giving the cottage a consistent decorative trim. Of all the cottages, this one had an unusual level of finish detail: tongue-and-groove knotty pine walls, woodwork and cabinetry detailing, a round brick fireplace, chair railing on the walls, and scalloped shingles on the original section's exterior. Bitty left the cove in 1969 and sold the cottage to her neighbors Laurie and Ken Gabriel. They added a spiral staircase in order to access the upstairs rooms from inside the house and enclosed the side porch to house a redwood hot tub that was "recycled" from Cottage #29.

When the Gabriels left, the cottage became one of six that sat empty and fell into disrepair after the state parks department stopped allowing new tenants to move in. Once the cottages on the north side of the beach have been restored, Cottage #11 will become an overnight rental.

TOP RIGHT:
Cottage #11 was one of the vacant cottages that caused controversy in the 1990s.

BOTTOM RIGHT:
Number 11 (oil on canvas, 36 x 48, 1978) by Bonnie Gregory.

BELOW:
Biddy Payne (kneeling in center, with hat on lap) and friends in front of Cottage #11, 1934.

Cottage #11

Cottage #15

The Whistle Stop

Sited on the corner where the entrance road meets the beach, the Whistle Stop, built in 1931, is one of the most prominent cottages at the cove. An early owner—Mr. Mitchell, a train engineer—gave the cottage its name and set up an electric model train that circled the Whistle Stop sign. After he died, Mrs. Mitchell moved to the Whistle Stop full time and modernized by moving walls, changing the location of the kitchen, and installing a forced-air heating system. You can still read the history of previous walls in the nail lines on the wooden floors. The most recent residents, Doug and Vivian Falzetti, added to that history with a decorative floor mural in the living room.

Thanks to its central location, the Whistle Stop was a natural gathering place. To keep the cove kids home on New Year's Eve, Doug and Vivian started an annual casino night that transformed the Whistle Stop into a gambling hall with blackjack and craps tables, a roulette wheel, and an arrow-shaped In-n-Out Burger sign, complete with flashing lights, letting people know that the party was on. Today #15 continues to be a social hub in its new incarnation as the Beachcomber Café.

RIGHT:
Doug Falzetti inside the Whistle Stop. In the final years at the cove Doug was its unofficial mayor, leading bridge and boardwalk maintenance projects and organizing get-togethers.

BOTTOM RIGHT:
Morning Path by Camille Przewodek (oil on canvas, 10 x 8, 2002).

BELOW LEFT:
Vivian's studio seen from the dining room, with one of her sculptures in the foreground.

BELOW:
Outside the Whistle Stop, 2004.

Cottage #15

The Future of Crystal Cove

By Laura Davick

Founder and Vice President, Crystal Cove Conservancy

"Once an isolated cove, now surrounded by a sea of urbanization. With your help, permanently preserved to inspire future generations forever."

The long road to today's park began shortly after the residents moved out. Once the resort plans had been halted, a two-year public review process, managed by the California State Parks Department, engaged stakeholders including myself and many others. In 2003, the California State Park and Recreation Commission and the California Coastal Commission adopted the Crystal Cove Preservation and Public Use Plan, defining the future use of the 46 historic cottages. The plan held at its core a commitment to public access and the preservation of the unique culture of the cove. Former residents could be assured that Crystal Cove would now remain much the way they remembered it.

The plan had four components — affordable overnight accommodations, education facilities, state park operations, and food services — that together would preserve the cove's history and ensure full public use and benefit. I envisioned building a new Crystal Cove community that would hold dear the spirit of the cove as I knew it and the vitality of the coveites I'd grown up with. This vision for an alternative to the resort plan included not only creating a place where families could come and experience Crystal Cove as the coveites had, but making it affordable, so that people from all walks of life could share this opportunity. It also included education facilities where visitors could learn more about this precious coastline, our fragile environment, the history of Crystal Cove, and the 100-year-long tradition of *plein air* painting at the beach. I traveled to many places in search of a model for reinventing Crystal Cove, but found no single place that matched this vision for what the new park could become. My collaborators and I would have to work together to invent a new model.

With the plan in place and broad public support behind it, the only missing piece was funding the project. Because the cove was now a state park, many taxpayers felt they'd already paid their share, but the state parks department had no funding to support the restoration of the cottages. Rather than let the project languish, the Alliance to Rescue Crystal Cove and Joan Irvine Smith threw a fundraising event for a parks bond measure, Proposition 40, supported by the Nature Conservancy Action Fund and scheduled to go before voters in early 2002. With the political connections of Joan Irvine Smith and the backing of community leaders like Mary Nichols and Sara Wan, we garnered the support of then-Governor Gray Davis and other state leaders, and the bond passed, providing the needed funding for much of the first phase of restoration at Crystal Cove. For the first time in years, we breathed a little easier knowing the cove was safe.

The Future of Crystal Cove

PREVIOUS PAGE:
Historic Crystal Cove remains timeless in modern Newport Coast.

ABOVE:
Crystal Cove's first cottage, #00, is now the Visitor Center.

RIGHT:
Student scientists collect ocean samples from the waters of Crystal Cove State Park.

The first phase of the project restored 22 of the cove's 46 historic cottages with a price tag close to $15 million. The project received the majority of funds, $11.2 million, from Proposition 40, as well as $2.9 million from mitigation funds from the California Coastal Commission.

When the cottages opened to the public on June 26, 2006, former coveites, state parks employees, and community members alike celebrated the unlikely preservation of the land and marveled at the remarkable way the cottages had been restored in every detail to the period of 1935 to 1955. Former residents entrusted us with original furnishings, photos, and memorabilia, which still reside in some of the cottages today and bring back much of the original spirit of the families who lived there.

Next, the dream of a Park and Marine Research Facility at Cottage #22 became a reality. We forged partnerships with institutions such as the University of California, Irvine and our education programs began to grow. In 2007, the Crystal Cove Historic District received the prestigious Governor's Award for Historic Preservation.

Since then, seven more cottages have been restored, including more overnight rentals, the Education Commons, the Beaches Film and Media Center in Cottage #13, and the historic garages, adding education and interpretive elements to the overnight rental program and further deepening our commitment to fulfilling the mission of preserving this unique place. None of this would have been possible without the generous support and donations we received, totaling $6.7 million.

These supporters, and all others to date, are proudly listed on the donor board inside Cottage #00, now known as the Crystal Cove Visitor Center.

The restored cottages are the perfect vehicle for passing on the magic of Crystal Cove to future generations. The cove's historic and natural resources are an irreplaceable outdoor classroom where thousands of students each year participate in citizen science programs. As a stewardship partner for Crystal Cove, we have been uniquely positioned to develop a nationally recognized STEM (science, technology, engineering, and math) education program that uses authentic field science and monitoring to immerse students and community members in the practices of conservation and open space management. By employing a social enterprise model that puts funds raised through overnight rentals and food service back into the park, we are working to ensure the community vision to avoid the "Disneyfication" of the cove in favor of preservation and public use. Through careful planning and generous support from numerous donors, private foundations, public revenue sources, and philanthropic investors, we have created the vision we wanted to see. Crystal Cove is now a model for how to fund important preservation, education, and conservation initiatives.

But our work is not finished. Today, in 2017, there remain 17 cottages on the north end of the beach that have not yet been restored. These precious historic resources are being battered by coastal wind and weather, falling further and further into disrepair. This shows how critically important preservation work can be: Without such efforts, we risk losing our history for good.

When restored, the last 17 cottages will become part of the overnight rental program, as well as a frontline laboratory for studying coastal engineering, sea level rise, and climate change. One of the cottages will serve as a dormitory-style lodge, hosting overnight education programs and helping build unbreakable bonds between students and our delicate coastline, creating in these young people the next generation of environmental stewards to care for our changing planet.

The restoration of these last cottages will double the number of available overnight rentals and create a lasting source of financial support for education and conservation efforts. Once all the cottages have been restored, the ongoing maintenance of the historic cottages will be 100 percent self-sustaining and will not require any additional funding from the state.

This will be the most ambitious phase of preservation work at Crystal Cove to date, but we know that it's possible when we look back at how much we and our partners have accomplished. Through the efforts of many, Crystal Cove will live on as a pocket of paradise for all of us to enjoy. Now surrounded by a sea of urbanization, it remains the tranquil bit of respite we need to sustain and empower our lives. Crystal Cove and other sacred public lands like it belong to all of us, and it is incumbent upon each of us to protect and preserve them. We invite you to participate in this ongoing effort. Our work is still before us, and we cannot do it without your support. Please join us in this endeavor and become part of the Legacy of Crystal Cove.

PREVIOUS PAGE:
The 17 cottages on the north beach of Crystal Cove, awaiting restoration.

RIGHT:
Stairway to paradise and the 29 restored cottages in the heart of the historic district.

FAR RIGHT, TOP:
Cottages on the north beach are currently closed to visitors.

FAR RIGHT, MIDDLE:
The porch of Cottage #4, which has been empty since 2001.

FAR RIGHT, BOTTOM:
A new generation discovers the tide pools just south of the historic district.

The Future of Crystal Cove

Crystal Cove Conservancy is a 501 c 3 nonprofit public benefit organization. The Conservancy was the first nonprofit organization to be awarded a concession contract to manage overnight rentals and food service at a California state park, a unique and successful model that continues today. With the cove protected and 29 of the 46 historic cottages restored, the Conservancy is dedicated to completing its final capstone project to preserve the last 17 cottages for future generations. We and our partners believe this will be our generation's legacy: to complete Orange County's greatest park and world-class outdoor classroom.

Crystal Cove Beach Cottages and Crystal Cove Management Company are wholly owned subsidiaries of Crystal Cove Conservancy. All proceeds are being re-invested back into the park to create a sustainable future for Crystal Cove State Park.

For more information, please visit www.CrystalCove.org.

Bibliography

Becker, Jack. *The California Impressionists at Laguna.* Old Lyme, CT: Florence Griswold Museum, Lyme Historical Society Inc., 2000.

Berkman, Leslie. "State Will Pay $32.6 Million for Coast Parkland." *Los Angeles Times.* December 5, 1979.

———. "Orange County's First 100 Years; Forging an Identity: The Irvine Saga." *Los Angeles Times* (Orange County Edition). May 22, 1988.

Blake, Janet, and Susan M. Anderson. *California Holiday: The E. Gene Crain Collection.* Laguna Beach, CA: Laguna Art Museum, 2002.

Brienes, Marvin, Bob Hare, and Eileen Hook. "Crystal Cove State Park Interpretive Plan." Sacramento, CA: Office of Interpretive Services, California Department of Parks and Recreation, 1985.

California Department of Parks and Recreation. "Crystal Cove Historic District Preservation and Public Use Plan." Sacramento, CA: 2003.

Calvert, Paul. "Flip Sea Lion Moves in on Beach Family." *Los Angeles Times.* March 24, 1964.

Chace, Paul G., Patricia A. Singer, Mark A. Roeder, and Wayne Bonner. "Of the Old Summer Fishing Camp: The Archaeological Heritage of ORA-1429, Los Trancos Canyon, Crystal Cove State Park." *Pacific Coast Archaeological Society Quarterly* 34 (2). Spring 1998.

Clinton, Paul. "Crystal Cove Residents File Suit." *Los Angeles Times* (Orange County Edition). February 14, 2001.

Cone, Marla. "Bridge over Troubled Cove Historical District." *Los Angeles Times* (Orange County Edition). April 12, 1991.

Earnest, Leslie. "Crystal Cove's Future Clouds Lives of Many." *Los Angeles Times* (Orange County Edition). April 11, 1990.

Elston, Bob. "Crystal Cove May Be Celebrating Its Last." *Los Angeles Times* (Orange County Edition). December 24, 1992.

Flagg, Michael. "Irvine Co. Heirs Are Finally Paid Quarter-Billion." *Los Angeles Times* (Orange County Edition). June 19, 1991.

Furlong, Tom, and Leslie Berkman. "Holdouts Stymied 100% Purchase of Irvine Co." *Los Angeles Times.* April 19, 1983.

Furlong, Tom and Debra Whitefield. "Irvine Co. Chief Comes under Attack by Smith, Ex-Official." *Los Angeles Times.* November 22, 1983.

Gamwell, Lynn. *West Coast Realism.* Laguna Beach, CA: Laguna Art Museum, 1983.

Gerber, Larry. "Paradise Lost; Crystal Cove Residents Must Bid Long Goodbye to Cherished Homes." *Los Angeles Times.* July 6, 1997.

Gerdts, William H., Jean Stern, Harvey Jones, and David Dearinger. *All Things Bright and Beautiful: California Impressionist Paintings from the Irvine Museum.* Irvine, CA: The Irvine Museum, 1998.

Goltz, James, Jan Decker, and Charles Scawthorn. "The Southern California Wildfires of 1993." EQE International. November 20, 1996.

Gottlieb, Jeff. "Crystal Cove Cottage-Dwellers Prepare to Board Up an Era." *Los Angeles Times* (Orange County Edition). March 4, 2001.

Bibliography

Haldane, David. "'Pocket Paradise' Crystal Cove a Quiet Hodgepodge of Old, Ramshackle Beach Shacks." *Los Angeles Times* (Orange County Edition). July 20, 1992.

Hall, Len. "Crystal Cove Dwellers Want to Delay Inevitable Eviction." *Los Angeles Times* (Orange County Edition). June 20, 1993.

Hall, Len. "Residents of Crystal Cove Win Eviction Reprieve for Another 2 ½ Years." *Los Angeles Times* (Orange County Edition). July 2, 1993.

Hofmann, Jan. "Marking Time, Crystal Cove Residents Maintain '30s Life Style Even as Tides of Development Rush Their Way." *Los Angeles Times* (Orange County Edition). November 19, 1988.

Ingram, Carl. "State Gives Final OK for Coast Parkland." *Los Angeles Times*. December 14, 1979.

Lesher, Dave. "Longtime Irvine Coast Antagonists Hail Agreement." *Los Angeles Times* (Orange County Edition). April 27, 1988.

Lynch, Rene. "Crystal Cove Tenants Face Another Day of Reckoning." *Los Angeles Times*. December 31, 1995.

———. "Tenants Sue State to Delay Evictions from Crystal Cove." *Los Angeles Times* (Orange County Edition). January 4, 1996.

———. "Luck Holds for the Dwellers of Crystal Cove." *Los Angeles Times* (Orange County Edition). July 9, 1996.

Mehta, Seema. "4 Sources of Crystal Cove Runoff Cited." *Los Angeles Times* (Orange County Edition). October 25, 2000.

———. "Ritzy Resort or Rustic Retreat?" *Los Angeles Times* (Orange County Edition). December 17, 2000.

———. "State Board OKs Crystal Cove Buyout." *Los Angeles Times* (Orange County Edition). March 23, 2001.

Moure, Nancy Dustin Wall. *California Art: 450 Years of Painting and Other Media*. Los Angeles, CA: Dustin Publications, 1998.

Moure, Nancy Dustin Wall, and Joanne L. Ratner. *A History of the Laguna Art Museum, 1918–1993*. Laguna Beach, CA: Laguna Art Museum, 1993.

Needham, John. "New Irvine Co. Plan for Coastal Development Wins Some Praise." *Los Angeles Times* (Orange County Edition). May 9, 1986.

Paddock, Richard C. "Politics Stall Evictions at Crystal Cove." *Los Angeles Times*. August 7, 1983.

Padve, Martha, and Christine F. Shirley. "National Register of Historic Places Inventory Nomination Form: Crystal Cove Historic District." Washington, D.C.: United States Department of the Interior, National Park Service. 1978.

Reyes, David. "Promise of Access to Crystal Cove." *Los Angeles Times* (Orange County Edition). October 21, 1997.

Saari, Laura. "A Woman of Valor: The widow of James Irvine III donated millions of dollars to charities and helped establish the University of California, Irvine." *Orange County Register*. May 25, 1993.

Schiesl, Martin. "Designing the Model Community: The Irvine Company and Suburban Development, 1950–88." *Postsuburban California: The Transformation of Postwar Orange County*. Edited by Rob Kling, Spencer Olin, and Mark Poster. Berkeley, CA: University of California Press, 1991.

Schoch, Deborah. "Project May Hurt Dolphin Habitat, OCC Biologist Says." *Los Angeles Times* (Orange County Edition). July 25, 1997.

———. "Resort Deal Is Questioned." *Los Angeles Times* (Orange County Edition). September 10, 1997.

———. "Crystal Cove Luxury Resort Contract Signed." *Los Angeles Times* (Orange County Edition). September 17, 1997.

———. "Crystal Cove Project Still on Track." *Los Angeles Times* (Orange County Edition). March 4, 1999.

———. "Light at the End of the Tunnel for Crystal Cove Activists." *Los Angeles Times* (Orange County Edition). September 16, 2000.

Shirley, Christine F. Private collection of materials relating to Crystal Cove. Pasadena, CA: n.d.

Smith, Joan Irvine, and Jean Stern. *Reflections of California: The Athalie Richardson Irvine Clarke Memorial Exhibition.* Irvine, CA: The Irvine Museum, 1994.

———. *California: This Golden Land of Promise.* Irvine, CA: The Irvine Museum, 2001.

Solon, Deborah Epstein. *Colonies of American Impressionism: Cos Cob, Old Lyme, Shinnecock, and Laguna Beach.* Laguna Beach, CA: Laguna Art Museum, 1999.

Stern, Jean. *Palette of Light: California Paintings from the Irvine Museum.* Irvine, CA: The Irvine Museum, 1995.

Stern, Jean, and William H. Gerdts. *Masters of Light: Plein-Air Painting in California 1890–1930.* Irvine, CA: The Irvine Museum, 2002.

Stern, Jean, Roy C. Rose, and Molly Siple. *Enchanted Isle: A History of Plein Air Painting on Santa Catalina.* Avalon, CA: Society for the Advancement of Plein Air Painting, 2003.

Vardon, Susan Gill. "Heiress Opposes Crystal Cove Resort." *Orange County Register.* January 17, 2001.

———. "Crystal Cove Plans Get Raucous Hearing." *Orange County Register.* January 19, 2001.

———. "Environmental Groups Unite to Fight Crystal Cove, Calif., Resort." *Orange County Register.* January 31, 2001.

———. "An Emotional Moving Out: Crystal Cove residents say goodbye, but cherish memories." *Orange County Register.* July 8, 2001.

Virginia Steele Scott Memorial Collection and *Examples from the Permanent Collection.* Laguna Beach, CA: Laguna Art Museum, 1980.

Westphal, Ruth. *Plein Air Painters of California: The Southland.* Irvine, CA: Westphal Publishing, 1982.

Whitaker, Barbara. "California Eyes Area Forgotten by Time." *New York Times.* March 18, 2001.

Wilson, Amy. "Crystal Cove Toasts Togetherness." *Orange County Register.* December 9, 1998.

Credits

All color photographs by John Connell except as indicated.
Collection of Joseph Ambrose Jr. and Michael D. Feddersen: 38, 104, 105
Courtesy Beatrice Anderson: 127
Courtesy Ken Auster: 39 bottom
Courtesy Meriam Braselle Collection: 2, 31 bottom, 45 top, 87 bottom
Courtesy Cynthia Britain: 36 top
Courtesy Pinky Brown: 73 bottom, 75 top and bottom, 81 top, 82
Courtesy the Buck Collection, Laguna Beach: 29 bottom
Collection of Jane Burzell: 112
Courtesy Saim Caglayan: 39 top
Photograph by Paul Calvert, courtesy Laura Davick: 78
Courtesy A.G. "Bud" Carter and family: 51 bottom, 55, 61, 66, 67 top left and top right
Photographs by Phillip Colla/oceanlight.com: 120, 123 top
Courtesy Cinda Combs: 143 bottom
Courtesy Carole Cooke: 63
Collection of Clifford D. and Louisa S. Cooper: 35 top right, 65 bottom left
Courtesy John Cosby: 17, 36 bottom, 119
Photograph by Peggy Darnell: 130
Courtesy Crystal Cove Conservancy: 149
Courtesy Laura Davick: 13 top right, 43 top, 46 bottom, 57, 59 bottom, 60, 71, 73 top, 83, 136 top and bottom
Photograph by Brian Day: 144 right
Courtesy the Falzetti family: 56, 65 bottom right, 68-69, 89 top, 129 top
Courtesy the Fenderson family: 72 top and center, 80, 81 bottom right, 84
Historical Collection-First American Corporation: 54
Photograph by Fred Emmert Air Views: 147
Courtesy the George Fuller family: 51 top; 58 top left, top right, and bottom left
Courtesy Laurie Gabriel: 142
Courtesy Jeffrey C. Horn: 40 bottom
Courtesy the Irvine Museum: 11 top and bottom, 27, 29 top, 35 bottom
Courtesy the Kinsella Library: 24-25
Courtesy Mary M. Kuntz-Coté: 100
Laguna Art Museum Collection, museum purchase with funds from prior gift of Lois Outerbridge: 31 top
Courtesy Laguna Art Museum: 33 top and bottom, 35 top left
Laguna Art Museum Collection, Gift of the Virginia Steele Scott Foundation: 97 top
Collection of the Laguna Canyon Foundation: 37
Photographs by J. Christopher Launi: cover, 148, 150-151, 152, 153 top, middle and bottom
Courtesy Calvin Liang: 6, 41
Photograph by John Malmin, Courtesy Pinky Brown: 76
Courtesy Marjorie and Douglas McClellan: 97 bottom
McCloskey Family Collection: 86, 113 top
Photograph by Pat McClure: 126
Courtesy Bob and Gen McMenomy: 44
Courtesy Jeannette Mellin: 58 bottom right
Photographs by Douglas Miller: 18-19, 22, 23, 42, 45 bottom, 90-91, 93 top, 96 right, 98-99, 101, 102, 103, 106, 108, 109 left
Courtesy Douglas Miller: 59 center
Diane Nesley Collection: 32
Courtesy Michael Obermeyer: 5, 15, 132 top right
Photograph by Jean Parker, courtesy Phyllis Parker Lowe: 70
Courtesy Jesse Powell: 9
Courtesy private collection: 28
Courtesy Camille Przewodek: 132 bottom, 145 bottom
Courtesy Richard Rice: 133 top
Courtesy Cinco and Edie Rowland: 115 left
Photographs by Rhea M. Sax: 118, 121, 122, 123 bottom, 125
Courtesy Virginia Sheeder-Mergell family: 47 bottom left and bottom right, 59 top left
Collection of Mrs. Christine F. Shirley: 48-49, 62
Collection of Rick Silver: 107
The Joan Irvine Smith Collection: 40 top, 133 bottom
Photographs by Bill Steen, courtesy the Steen family: 13 bottom right, 72 bottom, 74 bottom, 81 bottom left
Courtesy the Steen family: 74 top, 79, 93 center and bottom, 94-95
Courtesy George Strickland: 132 top left
Courtesy Jim Thobe: 96 left
Courtesy Ronald C. Wood: 52, 59 top right

Acknowledgments

More than its setting or architecture, Crystal Cove consists of the people who built it and brought it to vivid life. Without them, there would be no story to tell. We are deeply indebted to the families of Crystal Cove for generously sharing their personal stories and artifacts. Christine F. Shirley entrusted us with her extensive archive of materials, the basis of her own plans for a history of the cove. In many ways, this book is also hers. Martha Padve provided wisdom and insight, and for this we are grateful. For sharing their cherished memories—captured in both words and photographs—we offer our most profound thanks to Roger Armstrong and Alice Powell, Joan Baxter, Craig Benson, Sheree Benson-Ito, Barbara Boatman, Pinky and May Brown, Paul Calvert, A.G. "Bud" Carter and family, Cinda Combs, Pat Conners, Leo Dana and family, Peggy Darnell, Bob and Peggy Davick, the Stephen Davick family, Fletcher Dice, Jeanette Dillinger, Kevin and Mariana Donahue and family, the Falzetti family, the Fenderson family, Betty Ford McGraw, Pamela Freytag, the George Fuller family, Kenneth and Laurie Gabriel, Dorie Green, Sheila Green, Anne Hauser, Tim and Sharon Heintz, Stella Hiatt, the Hunter-Dickson-Barnard family, Sharon Jewett, John and Nancy Killen and family, the Ruth Kohlmeier-Van Wyck family, Charlotte Kortlander, Paul Kramer, Dave and Francois Levine, Carol Larsen and family, Homer Livermore, Kathy Livermore, Russ Makely, Rusty Makely, John Malmin, Don and Sally Martin, Marjorie and Douglas McClellan, the McCloskey-Burzell family, Zoe McCollum, Bob and Gen McMenomy, Jeannette Mellin, Bobby Mitchell, Brent and Peggy Ogden, Patti Ohslund, Phyllis Parker Lowe, John Paull, Ruth and Beatrice Pilaria and family, Shari Pilaria, Francine Rippey, Cinco and Edie Rowland, Rhea M. Sax, Peg Serenyi, Denise Serres, the Shatford family, the Virginia Sheeder-Mergell family, Walter Shirley, Elizabeth and Ruth Starr, Bill Steen and family, Sue Taallerud, Jim Thobe and Pam Gardiner, Mahlon Vail, Lee Van Pelt, Allan Wallace, Tom Webb, Robert Wentzel, and Ronald C. Wood. This book is our gift to them.

Crystal Cove is also beloved to many who never lived in the cottages, and the contributions of these individuals were essential to telling its story. John Connell donated generous amounts of his time to photographing the cottages and their residents; he has our gratitude. Douglas Miller, the unofficial historian of Laguna Beach, extended his scope to include Crystal Cove beginning in the mid-1970s. For the use of his vintage photography we offer heartfelt thanks. J. Christopher Launi has photographed Crystal Cove extensively; we are grateful for the use of his photos and for his continuing work to document the cove in the present day. We also thank Pat McClure for her photography, and Barbara Blankman of the First American Corporation for the use of their early historic images. We are indebted to marine biologist Dennis Kelly for his dolphin expertise, Phillip Colla for his underwater photography, and Ken Kramer of the California State Parks Department for his research of the marine environment and its historic artifacts. We are grateful to Lauren Carver from California state parks for her historic research on the Japanese schoolhouse and to the Honda family, who shared their history as members of the Japanese farming community. Thanks to Molly Siple and Lois Brown for sharing their publishing expertise. Brian Day brought his well-trained eye to the final stages of our project, for which we are grateful. We are indebted to Rick Lang, who photographed many of the paintings, and to Photo Smith for their excellent technical work on our digital images.

The artistic community of Orange County has been documenting—and thereby helping to preserve—Crystal Cove longer than anyone else. We must thank the early California *plein air* painters for coming to Laguna Beach in the late 1800s and starting what is now known as Laguna Art Museum to house their works and keep this history alive. We are thankful to the museum's former executive director, Bolton Colburn, as well as Janet Blake, curator of special collections/registrar, for sharing their knowledge and providing information and images for this book. Thanks also to Elaine and Peter Adams of the California Art Club for their support and for keeping the tradition of *plein air* painting alive.

We are especially appreciative of Joan Irvine Smith and her mother, Athalie Richardson Irvine Clarke, for their foresight in the collection of many of the earlier works of art in this book. Joan Irvine Smith has made known the importance of art as a tool in the preservation of history and has made it possible for current artists to thrive and thereby continue to act as what she calls "the preeminent environmental activists." We are thankful for the use of the many historic and current artists' images that she has lent to this book from her private collection. She and Jean Stern, the executive director of the Irvine Museum Collection at the University of California, Irvine have given freely of their time and expertise on our behalf.

Acknowledgments

Gallery owners David Hoy, Richard Challis, and Ray Redfern gave time, information, and images, for which we thank them. We extend our gratitude for the use of images to Tom Callis, registrar of the Orange County Museum of Art, the Bowers Museum, Laguna Art Museum, and the Irvine Museum, as well as the private collections of Richard Jahraus, the Laguna Canyon Foundation, Mary M. Kuntz-Coté, Joseph Ambrose Jr. and Michael D. Feddersen, Rick Silver, Diane Nesley, Gerald E. Buck, Clifford D. and Louisa S. Cooper, Don and Rosemary LaLonde, David Barnett, Hal Struck, Jay and Mary Linda Strocamp, and Constance Whitney.

We are grateful to all of the current artists from Laguna Plein Air Painters Association, California Art Club, Southern California Plein Air Painters Association and all of the other artists who have helped to document Crystal Cove over the years. For the generous loan of their artwork to this book, we thank Beatrice Anderson, Roger Armstrong, Ken Auster, Jacobus Baas, Kenn Backhaus, Cynthia Britain, John Budicin, Saim Caglayan, Val Carson, John Comer, Carole Cook, John Cosby, Vincent Farrell, Bonnie Gregory, Anita Hampton, Jeffrey C. Horn, Gregory Hull, Richard Kent, Calvin Liang, Michael Obermeyer, Alice Powell, Jesse Powell, Camille Przewodek, Richard Rice, Peggy Kroll Roberts, Junn Roca, W. Jason Situ, George Strickland, Jove Wang, and Steve (You-sui) Wang.

Laura thanks her grandparents, Guy and Mabel Webb, for first bringing their family to Crystal Cove in 1937. To her dearly beloved parents, Bob and Peggy Davick, who met at Crystal Cove and now rest off its shores, she offers thanks for teaching her that anything is possible. She is grateful to her brother, Stephen, and her sister, Susan, and for the wonderful childhood they shared growing up at Crystal Cove. To all of the "coveites," in honor of the idyllic lifestyle and memories that were made and shared, Laura thanks each of you for your invaluable contributions to this book. To Stella Hiatt, she is grateful for her love, lessons in living, and never-ending support. Laura also extends special thanks to Ken Kramer for his invaluable support and to Mike Tope for his wisdom and ongoing inspiration. Particular thanks to a treasured friend and mentor, Joan Irvine Smith, who has become a most valued advisor. For the generous financial contribution to initiate the writing of *Crystal Cove Cottages*, thanks to the California State Parks Foundation, the Crystal Cove Interpretive Association, Stella Hiatt, and Bob Flyte. Laura also thanks the cove's many generous supporters, including Crystal Cove Conservancy and Crystal Cove Beach Cottages staff, board members and volunteers who help bring Crystal Cove to life each day.

Meriam thanks John Connell, who had faith in this project from the inception, investing his time and expertise in the photography of the cottages with no guarantee of financial return. Thanks also to all of the coveites who shared their laughter, their tears, and their stories during the interview process. They welcomed us into their and hearts and homes, giving us a glimpse of their unique village lifestyle during their final days as residents at the cove. A sincere thank you to Cinda Combs (Meriam's original inspiration for doing the book), the Falzetti family, Stella Hiatt, Jane Burzell, the Barnards, Barbara Boatman, and the Thobe family. Meriam would like to express her appreciation to her fellow artists (especially the signature members of LPAPA) for supporting this effort as well as for allowing her to represent them during the coinciding quest for an art and cultural center at Crystal Cove. Thank you to Joan Irvine Smith for an education on art as well as politics and how to get things done. A special thanks to Janet Blake and Jean Stern for the continuing education on the early Laguna artists. Meriam is appreciative of her partners on the book, Laura Davick and Karen Steen, for joining her in this project and adding the energy and expertise to make it happen. She would like to dedicate her efforts on this project to her son, Clay, who spent the first five years of his life at Abalone Point in Crystal Cove State Park.

Karen thanks Horace Havemeyer III and *Metropolis* magazine for publishing her article on the cove and allowing her to reprint portions of it here. In particular she is grateful to Martin C. Pedersen for his mentorship and advice. Catherine Crawford, Criswell Lappin, and Nancy Nowacek graciously offered valuable professional opinions and technical assistance. Many thanks also to Laura and Meriam for the invitation to join this project. Karen sends her deepest love and appreciation to the Steen family, Devan Reiff, Linda Peters, and Andrea Vargo for their invaluable support and encouragement.

Finally, we thank Alan Rapp and Chronicle Books for their support and guidance in birthing the first book about Crystal Cove. And we are grateful to Randy Higbee and Harold Belmont for making this second edition of *Crystal Cove Cottages* possible.